D0614461

LIVING YOUR
HEART'S DESIRE

LIVING YOUR
HEART'S DESIRE

GOD'S CALL AND
YOUR VOCATION

GREGORY S. CLAPPER

UPPER
ROOM BOOKS®
NASHVILLE

Cover design: Lecy Design
Cover image: Jeff Baker / Taxi / Getty Images
Interior design: Nancy Terzian, nterdesign.com
First printing: 2005

LIBRARY OF CONGRESS CATALOGING-IN-PUBLICATION DATA
Clapper, Gregory Scott.
  Living your heart's desire : God's call and our vocation / by Gregory S. Clapper.
      p. cm.
  Includes bibliographical references.
ISBN 0-8358-9805-9 (pbk.)
1. Vocation.   I. Title.
  BV4740.C53 2005
  248.4—dc22   2004027637
            Printed in the United States of America

To DON E. SALIERS
and in memory of PAUL HESSERT

Two gentle mentors
and models
in the art of being a theologian—
one particular and peculiar
way to live out one's vocation

CONTENTS

ACKNOWLEDGMENTS

MY WIFE, JODY, has always been the first and last reader of my manuscripts, and she has once again been an invaluable help to me, suggesting several changes that I have incorporated into the final text. It was a delight to me that my daughters, Laura and Jenna, could also serve as readers for this book. Since they are both currently college students, their insights and comments on the theme of vocation were particularly helpful to me. Another college student, Charles Bruner, and two working ministers—Todd Outacalt and Charles Berdel—also read the manuscript. Dr. Jerome King Del Pino was a helpful respondent to the paper on vocation that I presented at the Oxford Institute of Methodist Theological Studies in 2002. Dr. Ellen Miller, a faculty colleague at the University of Indianapolis, after using my manuscript with a group of graduate students in physical therapy to reflect on their sense of vocation, provided helpful feedback. I also want to thank Dr. Leasha Schemmel for that regular, friendly prodding, "How is that vocation book coming?" Finally, I am indebted to the thoughtful and helpful editing of Jeannie Crawford-Lee.

The differing perspectives and comments that these various readers provided me improved my work greatly. During the last period of writing this book, I received a grant from the Crossings Project of the University of Indianapolis, for which I am appreciative.

INTRODUCTION

HUMAN TRANSFORMATION IS THE SOURCE OF ALL DRAMA. This is true for the artificial dramas of stage and screen as well as the real-life drama that makes our existence an adventure. Human transformation is, in the end, at the very heart of human life. The key question of life, then, is this: what kind of transformation will we embrace?

Christians believe that we are created to be changing in a particular way: our faith, love, joy, and peace should increase, while our fear, anger, hatred, and anxiety decrease. This kind of change—"spiritual growth," as it is sometimes called—is not to be identified completely with a onetime event, whether a conversion, a baptism, a confirmation, or any other mountaintop experience. Spiritual growth and change is to be the very stuff of the ongoing Christian life.

Often this question about the quality of our transformation lies in the background of life, with little of our conscious powers directed toward answering it. At other times, though, this question fights through all the background noise and becomes the central theme of life, demanding our focused attention.

Considering questions about our career can be such a time of focused attention, especially if we want our careers to fulfill a calling—to express a vocation—and not just be a job. This time of vocational discernment can come at many different points in life. For some, discernment will become particularly piquant as they approach their high school graduation. For others, it dawns as they enter college or as they move toward receiving their degree. For others it will come at midlife, and still others, as they face retirement. Some people will face a vocational crisis, perhaps shaded and colored in different ways, at all these phases of life.

Sometimes these deliberations arise from a mood of eager hope and excitement over the sheer unknown of an ill-defined but promising quest. At other times, pondering our work life can be occasioned by a dispiriting sense of burnout and deep disappointment. At still other times, it can develop out of a sense of ennui when the present reality is neither sweet nor bitter yet vaguely unsatisfying.

In my academic career, I have worked with a broad spectrum of high school, college, and seminary students. In my local church ministry, I interacted with a congregation that covered the whole age spectrum from birth through people in their nineties. Even though these groups represented all the different developmental stages, concerns, and attitudes one could imagine, in the end, on questions of vocation, all people have to deal with a basic set of issues. In this book I want to lift up and examine these common issues. I hope to help the reader embrace the kind of life-enhancing transformation that God in Christ invites us to embrace.

Billy Graham, as well as other ministers I respect, often say, "God has a plan for your life." I believe that is true: God's plan is to save us from our sins and to free us to help bring about God's reign on earth as it is in heaven, by living the fruit of the Spirit. However, that kind of plan differs from a treasure map with steps to the buried chest of gold; and I used to envision the "treasure map" kind of plan when I first heard Reverend Graham use that phrase. No, we get no treasure map for living out our vocation. But, to me, it seems infinitely better that instead we are given the gifts of human freedom and the Holy Spirit, who constantly invites us to use that freedom creatively.

One type of creative interaction between human freedom and the Holy Spirit can be seen in some expressions of the arts. For me the most evocative art form is film. In films we can see people stumbling, struggling, and responding to life creatively with the resources they are given. By being drawn into these struggles and seeing the creative responses that emerge, we the viewers can improve our own vocational discernment, taking inspiration from the lessons films offer. In each chapter I will make references to works of art, especially but not exclusively films. Filmmakers give us a rich and accessible set of images on which to reflect, vivid images that can enrich our own imaginations and, therefore, our lives. I will provide enough context for each film reference to make it meaningful even if you have not seen it. But if my comments invite you to view—or view again—any of these particular films, so much the better!

To suggest my intentions for this book, let me share a vignette about my own interaction with a film. A scene in the first *Star Wars* film stays alive in my memory. It's not one of the scenes that betray how the screenwriters borrowed from the Christian tradition, such as when Obi Wan Kenobi offers himself as a sacrifice so that the force may be strengthened and spread. I remember a less significant scene with a power for me nonetheless. A number of the laser-rifle-carrying rebel warriors are waiting, weapons ready, for a space station door to open. When that door opens, Darth Vader's troops will come pouring in, intent on the destruction of the rebel troops, Princess Leia, and the whole freedom-loving rebellion. The picture stands like a freeze-frame in my mind: the troops are ready for a challenge, both physically and mentally; they know an unknown summons to action lies on the other side of the door that is about to open … and they relish the confrontation.

When I first saw that scene, I wanted to be one of those troopers. Not in the sense of wanting to wreak mayhem and not in the sense of wanting to be the "star" (these troopers were mere extras, not the protagonists Luke Skywalker and Han Solo). No, what the troopers had that I wanted was something quite different. They had a mission. They had a focus for their energy. They had a purpose.

What lay ahead for those troops was not necessarily safe, and there were no guarantees of success—it was a risky enterprise. Yet it was one they embraced.

Perhaps some will recoil at this militaristic image. Just to be clear: my point is not to glorify war or violence, and joining the military is hardly the vocational answer for all people! Some people find their vocation perfectly expressed by suckling a baby, others by driving nails into wood, and others through a life of carefully driving the local school bus. The dramas of life and the vocations of faithful people are as varied as the flowers of the field and the birds of the air. What was compelling for me in this scene was the focus and dedication shown in the very postures of the soldiers, eagerly leaning into the ambiguous challenges before them.

Of course, imminent death does concentrate the mind wonderfully, as Samuel Johnson once remarked. Contemplating our mortality can provide a focus as few other things can. But something more compelling than the possibility of death on the other side of that door animated that scene in *Star Wars.*

What commands our full attention, enlivens us, and fills our hearts with the most exquisite longing is not just the possibility of facing death, not even finding something to die for. What commands our full attention is, instead, catching a vision of something to live for, however long or short that life may be.

Catching that vision is my goal for the readers of this book. Reading this book will not tell you which employment ads you should answer or even which career will be best for you. I seek something more foundational. I want you to be able to lead a life of Christian faithfulness in all realms of existence. While elements of epic drama may occur in such a life (as in *Star Wars*), there are also inescapable elements of comedy—even farce—as well as tragedy and heartbreak. Leading a life of Christian vocation will almost certainly not always be what you thought it would be, and at times it probably will not be what you want it to be. It will, though, be the life that satisfies your deepest heartfelt longing. It will be the life worth living.

What gear do we need for this adventure? I will not try to provide an exhaustive inventory up front. As players do

Be honest in your awareness of who you are.

in some video games, we will discover many of the resources along the way. I would simply ask you to bring one reality to the forefront of your awareness as we begin—a humble and honest openness about who you are. Not who you *should* be according to various voices in society but the real, private awareness about yourself when no one except you is looking or asking. Whether you come to a season of vocational discernment like my bright-eyed dogs when they lay the tennis ball at my feet—eager, focused, and excited—or come to the task dragging and limping—feeling mortally wounded from the battlefields of life—be honest in your awareness of who you are.

Far from clearing everything up, having such an awareness may mean confronting more questions and opening up more uncertainties. Believe it or not, that is a good sign. Just as having an appetite for food signals health, having a sense of how provisional and uncertain your present answers are can signal spiritual health, indicating you are ready for the journey. After all, Jesus said that it is those who hunger and thirst for being related to God who will be filled—not those who already think they are full (Matt. 5:6).

CHAPTER **ONE**

"I'M NO GOOD AT BEING NOBLE"

CHRISTIAN VOCATION
IN A CYNICAL WORLD

Being Called
in a Culture of Irony

People often choose to take a sarcastic, cynical, bitter, and detached approach to life. It has been a perennial human option. We find this approach given voice by the jaded author of Ecclesiastes, who describes life as "vanity of vanities! All is vanity" (1:2). As Eugene Peterson puts this passage in his brilliant Bible translation *The Message*, "There's nothing to anything—it's all smoke." In other words, "Been there, done that, got the T-shirt." "Whatever."

The option for this attitude should come as no surprise to Christians, since the story of the Fall says that our sin has separated us from God. We are alienated. *Alienation* is a fancy word for what can be expressed through either the passive indifference of the resigned shrug or the active hostility of the raised middle finger. Sarcasm and cynicism, though differing from each other in important ways, are attitudes born of such alienation. Alienation distances us from the issue at hand; it lets us stand off, judge, and mock. In one way or another, such an attitude proclaims that the present topic of discussion/state of affairs/condition of life does not capture the speaker's full allegiance.

Now, being able to distance ourselves from certain realities can be a useful skill in our repertoire. At times we do need to separate ourselves from—and even mock—error and folly when they threaten to cloud our vision of the truth. In our culture, however, cynical irony has become not the defender of truth but an end in itself, the primary idiom. Mockery of values, not for the sake of higher values but simply for its own sake, characterizes much of our contemporary world. Only noncommitment preserves the mockers from being mocked themselves. "Whatever" is the catchall response because it does not matter what question is asked or what response is elicited; the attitude of indifference will remain unchanged. "You can't make me care."

This culture's crust of cynicism, sometimes expressing sarcasm and even bitterness, will encase us if we are not proactive against it, as Christians must be. This crust challenges the Christian life, for when everything is a joke, nothing is worth giving one's life to, much less giving one's life for. Being "called," by contrast, means setting your heart and mind—your entire life—toward one goal. Answering a call means getting up out of the scoffer's seat and walking out on the playing field. Being called means making a vulnerable and risky assertion of one's whole life. And Christians are called.

THE CALLING OF CHRISTIANS

Call, from the Latin word *vocare*, "to call," is the root meaning of *vocation*. Many think of God's calling as primarily related to a particular job, but this is a crucial misunderstanding. Our culture has debased the word *vocation* to an association almost exclusively with the way one earns money, but in the Christian context, a calling or "vocation" is not a career. Scripture gives us a larger and more empowering sense of calling.

Ephesians 1:17-19 speaks of knowing "the *hope* to which [God] has called you" (italics added), and Ephesians 4:4 echoes this same phrase—that God calls us to hope. In John 6, where the people ask Jesus what they are to do "if our work is to be the work of God" (v. 28),

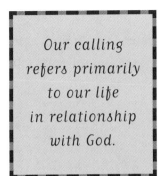

Our calling refers primarily to our life in relationship with God.

Jesus replies, "This is the work that God requires: to believe in the one whom he has sent" (v. 29, REB). To see our "calling" put in terms of *hoping* and *believing* starkly shows us that we will go hopelessly wrong from the start if we take our cue from culture and see our "calling" as primarily related to a job or career. Our calling refers primarily to our life in relationship with God.

To be sure, *hoping* and *believing* in the God Christ revealed will lead to all manner of commitment, involvement, and energy expenditure. Scripture explicitly names examples of this kind of energy expenditure. Jesus says feeding the hungry, providing shelter to the homeless, and visiting the sick are services rendered to Christ himself (Matt. 25:31-46). It is true that some particular jobs, and even entire careers, can flow from a call. But our real job in life is much wider than any career.

Ephesians 4:1 tells us we are to "lead a life worthy of the calling to which you have been called." That passage goes on to list some specific expressions of this "worthy life." These particular examples of the worthy life flow from God's gifting

> *You do not have to be an apostle, a prophet, or a pastor to express the calling of God.*

of the people: "Some would be apostles, some prophets, some evangelists, some pastors and teachers, to equip the saints for the work of ministry, for building up the body of Christ" (vv. 11–12). Here we find the image of the different parts of the "body of Christ" functioning together in order for the whole to work properly. (Paul used the same vivid metaphor of the body to refer to all believers in Romans 12 and 1 Corinthians 12.)

Reading this biblical list of worthy jobs might lead us to think that only those tasks specifically mentioned are worthy expressions of our calling. However, the same chapter offers more general advice to all disciples, independent of whether they embrace one of these explicitly named "callings." Oddly enough, this advice comes through an admonition to thieves. "Thieves must give up stealing; rather let them labor and work honestly with their own hands, so as to have something to share with the needy" (v. 28). In other words, you do not have to be an apostle, a prophet, or a pastor to express the calling of God. Anyone doing honest work can follow God's call by giving to the needy.

However, another misunderstanding of Christian calling can arise from reading this passage: putting a check in the offering plate fully discharges our call. God wants much more than that, and in our heart of hearts, we want to give much more than that.

Ministers or priests and regular financial givers to the building fund are not the only ones who have callings. *All* Christians have a calling—the call to God. No circumstances of the job market or national economy can keep us from fulfilling that calling. That truth implies that a particular focus of our energy—whether a job, career, or particular tasks or duties—can be *consistent with* our calling or an expression of our calling but can never be *identical to* our calling. As Os Guinness has pointed out in his book *The Call: Finding and Fulfilling the Central Purpose of Your Life*, Christians are not called primarily to *do something* or *go somewhere*; we are called *to Someone.*[1] That is what we are to be single-minded about—walking a path in faith and hope that leads us to God.[2] No particular geographical location, state of health, or quality of the job market can hinder us from following that call—if following that call is our heart's true desire.

GOD'S CALL AND CULTURE'S SARCASM

God's call is ours to embrace but not in an isolated Christian ghetto, sealed off from the rest of reality. We are to live out our calling in the wider world that is God's creation. This means we cannot hide our calling and shelter it from the larger ironic and cynical culture. Having a clear calling at the center of our lives opens Christians to the acidic sarcasm of those who do not have something to give themselves to. We must live our calling and proclaim the gospel in a world that will greet it with mockery.

It can be some small comfort to know that the "mockers" were all too familiar to Jesus (see Matt. 20:19; 27:27-44).

> We must live our calling and proclaim the gospel in a world that will greet it with mockery.

Perhaps, in certain circumstances, encountering mockery can even serve as a kind of spiritual Geiger counter: the higher the readings we are picking up from society, the closer we might be to living out our call! (We need humility in such circumstances, however, to keep us from spiritual self-congratulation and pseudo-martyrdom in every perceived slight.)

Besides girding ourselves with this scriptural reassurance, we need to understand just how deeply our culture is saturated with sarcasm if we are to prevail against such an onslaught. This sarcasm distorts our very perceptions of reality. We especially need to recognize how it can distort our understanding of what it means to work. In doing so, we will also see how a sarcastic and mocking attitude often conceals powerful spiritual yearning, which finally can be answered only by responding to the very call of God it mocks.

THE CRUST OF SARCASM IN OUR CULTURE

When Christians are sorting out what to "do with their lives," we must fight through this culture of sarcasm; we must break through the "crust" of sarcasm in which our culture tries to trap us. This culture fosters ideas about work and vocation that will keep us from our holy calling if we let them form our hearts.[3]

The popular press has been conscious of the fact that Western culture (especially the culture of the United States, which sets the tone for much of the world) has been an ironic and often cynical one. While we might think this is a recent phenomenon, in fact it is one of the enduring themes of twentieth- and twenty-first-century art and culture. Indeed, much of the twentieth-century world of art mirrors the distancing, sarcastic attitude of our culture. Indicative of that connection, Richard Schickel titled his turn-of-the-century retrospective on the arts in the twentieth century in *Time* magazine "The Arts: 100 Years of Attitude."[4]

One book that vividly portrays this jaded view of life, while also holding out hope for something more, has been required reading in American high school English classes for more than fifty years and has become a modern classic. This is *The Catcher in the Rye* by J. D. Salinger. The protagonist, teenager Holden Caulfield, struggles to find a place in a world full of "phonies." In a conversation where he rejects career options such as being a scientist or a lawyer, he reveals his ideal occupation (which was inspired by his mishearing of a Robert Burns poem). He says:

> Anyway, I keep picturing all these little kids playing some game in this big field of rye and all. Thousands of little kids, and nobody's around—nobody big, I mean—except me. And I'm standing on the edge of some crazy cliff. What I have to do, I have to catch everybody if they start to go over the cliff—I mean if they're running and they don't look where they're going I have to come out from somewhere and catch

> them. That's all I'd do all day. I'd just be the catcher
> in the rye and all. I know it's crazy, but that's the
> only thing I'd really like to be. I know it's crazy.[5]

In a world populated with phonies, Holden wants to save little kids from destruction. The cynical, empty world of the phonies would see this vocation as "crazy" (as he emphasizes twice), but that is what he wants to do.

Many popular films depict this conflict when individuals are pulled in a higher direction while the world drags them down. We see a classic story of worldliness and deadening irony masking a deeper hunger in *Casablanca*, considered by many critics one of the best films ever made. In this film, Rick, an American living in exile in Casablanca, is supporting himself by running a café and casino. The epitome of the hard-boiled, cynical, world-weary man, his primary idiom is irony. Rick's steely aloofness—"He never drinks with customers"—vanishes, however, when the woman who broke his heart, Ilsa, comes back into his life.

When Ilsa tells Rick the real reason she had to leave him years ago—a departure that broke his heart—his old, embittering interpretation of her is transformed. Her revelation reconfigures his own past. With the blinders of bitterness removed, he once again looks to a wider, more fulfilling vision of life. In the movie's climactic scene, Rick is about to sacrifice his personal, romantic happiness and send his lover out of the country with her husband—clearly a noble response to a call higher than his own self-seeking. He opens with a memorable phrase addressed to Ilsa, "I'm no good at being noble, but . . ."

This denial of nobility suggests Rick's lingering desire
to be considered the humble,
unpretentious "everyday Joe."
He does not want to open himself up to the caustic cynicism
of which he has been such an

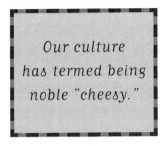

*Our culture
has termed being
noble "cheesy."*

expert practitioner. He is willing to live a higher calling but
uncomfortable with claiming to do so. That would draw
mocking sarcasm. Our culture has termed being noble
"cheesy." It seems self-dramatizing and leaves one open to
that pseudodemocratizing accusation: "Who do you think
you are?"

In claiming a calling, then, we choose to be vulnerable to such stings, to say no to being forever cool and aloof.
In the eyes of the world, trying to live out a calling is
"crazy," as Holden Caulfield emphasizes, and Rick wants to
be regarded as "no good" at it. But these characters, like
the gospel, proclaim that only a life of commitment leads
to fulfillment.[6]

Being noble in this sense, though, does not equate with
credulity or innocence. Nor does it mean being merely
earnest or sincere. Being noble in this sense implies claiming a classic Christian virtue—simplicity.[7] Not simple as in
"simpleminded," though the practitioners of sarcasm usually try to foster that connection. The cynical scoffers like
to characterize those who follow a calling as lacking the
intelligence to live ironically distanced from the world. They
consider anyone who eschews floating above the life of

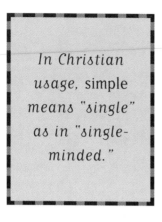

> *In Christian usage,* simple *means "single" as in "single-minded."*

commitments as suckers, saps, dorks, or nerds.

In Christian usage, *simple* means "single" as in "single-minded." The Danish thinker Søren Kierkegaard said purity of heart is to will one thing. The double-mindedness of the ironic and sarcastic must give way to the singleness of purpose of the pure in heart. To will one thing—namely, faithfully following our calling—may mean that at times we are swimming upstream. But when we are following our calling, we will have the one thing that can sustain us against any current: we will know that we are swimming toward home.

When Rick in *Casablanca* reawakened to both human suffering and the possibility of lessening that suffering, he resumed that swim toward home. Discovering that Ilsa had acted nobly rather than deceitfully when she left him years ago allowed Rick to take a fresh look at reality, forget himself and his heartbreak, and take up the fight against the Nazis. Dropping his distanced, ironic stance born of self-pity, he sees the suffering of the world vividly and quickly identifies a role for himself in lessening that suffering. He gives up life as a self-seeking, jaded casino owner and puts his life at risk in the wider world at war. Joined by his fellow former cynic, the chief of police, the two walk off into what could be the beginning of a "beautiful friendship"—that uniquely powerful kind of friendship that forms between individuals who gladly throw themselves into the risky life of living out a calling.[8]

CLAIMING OUR LONGING FOR MEANINGFUL WORK

Encountering the reality of suffering and human need can have a variety of effects, depending on the shape of your heart at the time you encounter it. If you have a heart formed by the gospel, encountering suffering and need can inflame your desire to commit your energy to a cause and spur transformative activity in God's creation. As a minimal beginning to the process, encountering suffering can crack the crust of sarcasm, which otherwise deafens us to our calling.

Reflecting on one of the most notable examples of the brokenness and suffering in the world, the terrorist attacks of September 11, 2001, *Time* columnist Roger Rosenblatt wrote an essay called "The Age of Irony Comes to an End."[9] A few months later, Lance Morrow, also of *Time*, lifted up for praise the work of American film director Frank Capra. Capra's work was marked by assertion of Christian values, and he was sometimes mocked as producing "Capra-corn." Even though Capra produced his work sixty years before Morrow wrote, Morrow declared that Capra's "theme of common-man decency vs. phoniness has a contemporary ring."[10]

Understanding the power of an encounter with brokenness and suffering to shake us out of a cynical attitude is hardly a recent insight. John Wesley, the eighteenth-century Christian reformer, often told societies of Methodists to *visit* the poor rather than just give money to the poor. Wesley knew that in visiting the poor, Methodists could not help but meet the reality of suffering in a compelling and life-changing way. *Visiting, seeing,* and *encountering* human suffering and need will break us out of the crust of jaded sarcasm like nothing else."

SUFFERING, HUMAN NEED, AND OUR CALLING

Here, though, we have to confront a hard truth: suffering is repellent. It seems like a cosmic mistake and, hence, something to be downplayed, avoided, or suppressed. When, as a young man, I started investigating questions about God, getting away from the messiness of the world and its brokenness and suffering appeared to be the most promising route to get clear about God. If I could just filter out that kind of "noise," I could perhaps isolate the true "signal" that God must be sending out. Imagine my shock when I found out that God's "signal"—God's call—comes to us in the midst of that broken and confusing welter of suffering that is life in the world! If we try to abstract ourselves from all that suffering and brokenness in order to find God, we can only find (as Kierkegaard said) an abstraction for a God that can relate to us only if we become an abstraction ourselves.

As I described in *When the World Breaks Your Heart*, suffering and tragedy provided a way into the heart of God for me. But I have no intention of romanticizing or sentimentalizing this experience. When we encounter suffering firsthand, see it up close in the lives of friends or family, or view it in news of a distant land, it is an undeniably repulsive, dispiriting, and heartbreaking reality. Certainly, in many ways, suffering should legitimately be prevented or avoided if at all possible. And yet, God calls to us through suffering and even—most unexpectedly— God calls us to enter into suf-

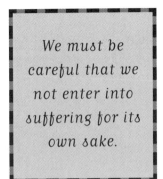

We must be careful that we not enter into suffering for its own sake.

fering. That concept scandalizes the speculative philosopher who seeks a neat, stoically defensible "theism." But, as Paul styled it, to those who are called, this way of life marked by entering into the suffering of the world, the way of life exemplified by Christ on the cross, is "the power of God and the wisdom of God" (1 Cor. 1:24).

We must be careful first of all, though, that we not enter into suffering for its own sake, like the misguided monks of the Middle Ages who would whip themselves in the name of spiritual growth. Our ultimate destination is not suffering but the realization of our hope in God. If God calls us to suffering, we must follow that call, just as we follow the call when it leads us to pleasure. The pain and the pleasure are not themselves the point. Faithfulness is.

Secondly, the Christian tradition clearly affirms that the suffering and sin of the world can be effectively confronted only with grace. Opening ourselves to the world's brokenness before arming ourselves with the resources God makes available can lead not to a rich spiritual life but to discouragement and despair. Suffering, like temptation, does not carry its own antidote; we require resources outside our immediate experience to deal with it. Christians, then, must live in that sometimes-painful place where neither embracing nor ignoring suffering is an option. Our only option is working to alleviate suffering with the help of God's grace.

Ours is the humble task of seeing what is real—suffering included—and trying to live our vocation in the midst of this broken reality. The gospel directs us to honor the longing within us, the longing to make a significant difference in the world, the longing seen in Holden Caulfield of *The Catcher in the Rye* and Rick of *Casablanca*, and in so many other cultural expressions.[12] If we do not honor this longing, our work—indeed, all of our energy expenditures in our jobs or elsewhere—will show that we have stopped listening for the call God gives us through Jesus Christ.

We can construe vocation as a call to help spread the kingdom of God on earth as it is in heaven—our regular petition in the Lord's Prayer. The following chapters will explore what it means to work for God's kingdom to come in our day and time.

Questions for Reflection and Discussion

1. Consider the proposal that our culture promotes cynicism, irony, and sarcasm. Does this ring true for you? If so, in what ways have you encountered the scoffer's mocking attitude? Why do you think people adopt this attitude?

2. Reflect on what you have understood the concept of "Christian vocation" to mean. Was it primarily related to a job or career? What changes in your life or attitudes would you make if you understood your vocation as a call to Someone rather than a call to a particular job or place?

3. Consider what happens when someone with an ironic, distancing attitude of noncommitment encounters the call to Christian commitment, particularly the idea of living out a "calling." What examples of such an encounter do you recall in your own life or the lives of others? Try to think of an example in which the cynical attitude of our culture won an individual's allegiance and another in which the Christian calling won a person's commitment.

4. Reflect on your own experience of encountering suffering, either your own or that of others. Do you push suffering out of awareness, or is it a part of your everyday life? If you are usually aware of suffering, how do you deal with it? Does it lead to anxiety? guilt? anger? prayer? depression? action?

5. When you think about the reality of suffering, do you see it as being taken care of by professionals who deal with "that sort of thing," or do you see your life as more personally and intimately engaged with the broken and messy parts of life? Especially if you are not in one of the helping professions (doctor, nurse, clergy, therapist, etc.), consider how the world's suffering and God's call to live in God's kingdom can be a part of your everyday vocation.

CHAPTER TWO

THE GOSPEL AND WORK

Misunderstandings about Christianity

The biggest and most common misunderstanding regarding Christianity is to see it as all about being good.

All too often people think Christianity's first (or only) proclamation is: "Be good." This emphasis (which is not unknown even within Christian circles) implies that the practice of Christianity centers on will—on *doing*, and more specifically, doing "good." In fact, though, the gospel primarily declares something entirely different. Christianity at its pulsating core proclaims: "Be loved."

The "good news" is that the God who created us is the God who forgives us, loves us, and calls us to a life of love. The gospel recognizes our dual tendency: to put ourselves at the center of the universe but also to be profoundly uncomfortable in that position. When we hear and heed the call to be loved, we can heave a sigh of relief and realize we don't hold reality together by our efforts; we don't have to spend ourselves creating and defending a self-image. God has given us our self-image as a free gift; we are created in the image of God, and we are forgiven sinners. God has called us into being; we are not our own creator; and we are not expected to be our own redeemer.

The gospel, then, at its essence, at its first logical moment, does not concern *doing* at all but *being*. It is about receiving, being open to hear with the center of who we

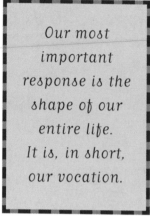

Our most important response is the shape of our entire life. It is, in short, our vocation.

are—our "heart" in biblical language—that we are precious in the eyes of our Creator.

Of course, this proclamation of God's love and forgiveness does call for a response. Our will does come into the Christian picture but not as an initiating force imposing itself on reality and creating meaning (as some existentialists and a few misguided Christians see it). Our will comes into the picture when we *respond* to this word of love.

Our response to this proclamation of love and forgiveness cannot be exhaustively defined by going forward in church at the end of a service—answering an "altar call"—or saying a prayer of commitment around a campfire at a church retreat. Those acts can significantly affect the lives of individuals, but they do not constitute the whole story of Christian response. Our most important response is the shape of our entire life. It is, in short, our vocation.

The second most common misunderstanding of Christianity is the exact opposite of the first misunderstanding. This misunderstanding assumes Christianity has nothing to do with being good. "I am saved and I know I am going to heaven" is the rallying cry of this view. Such a declaration implies that going to heaven is the complete message of the gospel, except perhaps for the need for evangelism—that is, getting others to heaven. Coupling this theology with an attitude of imminent apocalypticism (such as that fostered by the *Left Behind* series) makes life like a giant waiting room—boring at best, nightmarish at worst. There people chatter about what it will be like when they get out of this place and get to the location of ultimately important action.

For those laboring under the first misunderstanding of Christianity—that focuses exclusively on doing the right thing—life can seem like a dry, grind-it-out exercise in staying power. Eternal salvation depends on anxiously controlling human efforts. Given the opposite misunderstanding—that doing good has nothing to do with Christianity—life and creation are a gray netherworld, a necessary but bothersome interlude before the Real Thing. Because both these misunderstandings are prevalent, it should be no surprise that people often suffer confusion when they try to live their total life, including career, as an expression of a call from God.

We need to recognize an important (if theologically subordinate and reactive) role for human exertion, for the active use of our will—in short, for *doing*—once we are called into the life of humble forgiveness, love, and joy by the gospel. Understanding the nature of work puts the correct view of Christian doing into relief. Gilbert C. Meilaender has laid out a profound typology of four different views of the nature of work. This typology can aid Christians in understanding and living out our callings. It also enables us to break through our culture's crust of call-deadening irony and cynicism.

UNDERSTANDING WORK

In his book *Working: Its Meaning and Its Limits,*[1] Gilbert C. Meilaender presents a collection of readings on the meaning and function of human work, play, and rest. He spells out four understandings of work: work as cocreation, work as necessary for leisure, work as dignified but irksome, and work as vocation.

To understand work as cocreation, Meilaender starts by quoting Genesis 1:26-31. Here we see that humans are created in the image of God and are called to "be fruitful and multiply, and fill the earth and subdue it; and have dominion over the fish of the sea and over the birds of the air and over every living thing that moves upon the earth" (Gen. 1:28). This passage speaks to the idea that our activities are not to be those of a puppet. Instead, we are to spend our energy in a way analogous with God. Activities like "being fruitful and multiplying," "subduing," and "having dominion" rely on our creativity, which relates to our being created in the image of the ultimate Creative One.

Interestingly, when Meilaender addresses the second view of work—work as necessary for leisure—he does not find a suitable scripture to quote. He does find, however, suitable passages from Hesiod and Aristotle. According to this view, work holds value primarily because it allows for leisure. Working just enough to obtain leisure is the proper goal from this perspective.

The Christian might object to this conception because the point of life according to scripture is not to get by with spending as little energy as possible but to spend our energy well. However, if we see leisure not as mere "idleness" (the opposite of "work" in William J. Bennett's *The Book of Virtues: A Treasury of Great Moral Stories*) but instead as opportunity to pursue more fulfilling activities, this view could lead to profoundly Christian visions of life and worship.[2]

When elaborating the view of work as "dignified but irksome," Meilaender quotes Genesis 3:8-19, which speaks of work after the Fall as "toil." He also makes reference to 1 Thessalonians 4:10b-12, which commands Christians to work with their hands and be dependent on nobody. Further, 2 Thessalonians 3:6-12 instructs Christians to keep away from anyone living in idleness; if anyone will not work, that person will not eat. Here work is not shameful, but that does not make it pleasant.

GOD'S CALL—PARTICULAR BUT NOT RIGID

When discussing his fourth category—understanding work as vocation—Meilaender quotes 1 Corinthians 7:17 ("only, let everyone lead the life which the Lord has assigned to him, and in which God has called him"). He also turns to classical Protestant sources on vocation, such as Calvin's *Institutes of the Christian Religion* and William Perkins's *A Treatise of the Vocations or Callings of Men*.

Regarding work-as-calling, Meilaender cites John Wesley as the archetype of "diligent, methodical labor in one's calling" (p. 11). This view of work as calling is, according to Meilaender, the typical Protestant view, captured by C. S. Lewis's assertion that the Christian is to focus not on doing good works but on doing good *work* (p. 12).

Meilaender also quotes Charles Wesley's hymn "Forth in Thy Name, O Lord." The first two stanzas of Wesley's hymn give us, in the condensed idiom of the poet, a sense of this typically Protestant understanding:

Forth in thy name, O Lord, I go,
my daily labor to pursue;
thee, only thee, resolved to know
in all I think or speak or do.

The task thy wisdom hath assigned,
O let me cheerfully fulfill;
in all my works thy presence find,
and prove thy good and perfect will.

Charles Wesley believes God calls individuals to a particular job ("The task thy wisdom hath assigned"), *yet* the primary, universal calling of all Christians *to* God should fundamentally determine the course of human life ("thee, only thee, resolved to know in all I think or speak or do").

Many Christian writers now consider this point of view—that all humans are called to a particular job or career—a mistake.[3] As with many mistakes, we can understand it by looking at the historical context in which it arose. Specifically, this interpretation of vocation arose from Martin Luther's legitimate rejection of the medieval Roman Catholic view that only the priests, monks, and nuns had a vocation—a calling from God. Luther held that all people had a "station" in life that they were meant—by God—to fill. The stable hand was fulfilling his call just as the local prince on his throne was fulfilling his call. A reassuring view—especially for the prince!

Modern Christians, especially those who grow up in Western democracies, see society and career possibilities as quite a bit more flexible than Luther could in his feudal world. Luther did Christians a great service by freeing "vocation" from a rigid clerical paradigm. But to see God's calling to us as primarily active in the economic realm, the realm of making money necessary to live, is an equally egregious error. We should feel no need to follow either Luther or Charles Wesley on this point.

> *It is important for Christians to acknowledge that work can indeed be irksome and at times functions as no more than a means to obtaining leisure.*

CHRISTIANS AND THE FOUR VIEWS OF WORK

Meilaender certainly attributes an exalted role to two types of work—work as cocreation and work as vocation. He does us a favor, however, by listing and discussing the other two categories as well, showing that in some parts of our lives—perhaps even in our dream job—work has only a limited spiritual significance.

While we can easily romanticize work and emphasize the more exalted depictions of it, it is important for Christians to acknowledge that work can indeed be irksome and at times functions as no more than a means to obtaining leisure. If we humbly acknowledge these realities, perhaps

> *Leading a life of jaded detachment from the world leads to a refusal of the vocation we were created for.*

we can avoid the unnecessary guilt that results from considering cocreation and vocation to be the only work experiences worthy of good Christians. We know that ennobling and inherently worthwhile work does not tell the whole story of our energy expenditures.

However, if the *Christian* needs to keep in mind this wider perspective—acknowledging that not all work qualifies as cocreation or a direct expression of God's call—the *worldly* person, in contrast, needs to hear the opposite word. The secular scoffer needs to hear the good news that sometimes work can be more than simply irksome or a means to enjoy the weekend. Leading a life of jaded detachment from the world leads to a refusal of the vocation we were created for and constitutes a primary rebellion against our Creator. If we allow the world to form us in this way, more than likely we will come to see work as irksome or only a means to leisure. When that happens, the longing given voice by *The Catcher in the Rye*'s Holden Caulfield and Rick of *Casablanca* will go unanswered.

These multiple visions of work raise important questions: How can we depict a single vision of the Christian life true to both the promise of rewarding work and the reality of deadening and merely instrumental work? How can we express the vision of a more fulfilling way of life in terms compatible with our experience and with the Christian tradition? How can we find reasonable hopes for realizing our vocation when the evidence in the real world for this possibility seems shaky at best? To these questions I will turn in the following chapter. But before we pursue those questions, let us close this chapter with a reminder of the context for *all* of our working.

BEING, DOING, AND THE GOSPEL

Remembering that God's love first called us into being and into salvation, we can perhaps see the extension of that call to be work amid God's creation. Our work is not the logically primary feature of our Christian lives—our work is instead a joyful response of thanksgiving and gratitude for all God has done and all God is. This gratefulness explains why prayers of thanksgiving come to a Christian's lips so often and why communal worship—shaped as it is by praise and thanksgiving—defines the gathered Christian community. We call the order of worship for such gatherings the *liturgy,* which means "the work of the people."

The conclusion of a popular and critically acclaimed film illustrates this dynamic relationship between our being and our doing. I will apply some reinterpretation for a completely Christian understanding. In *Saving Private Ryan,* a group of soldiers is sent out to bring home a soldier whose brothers have all been killed. The government has decided that having one family lose three sons in World War II was enough and that the surviving son—the Private Ryan of the title—should be brought home before he too is killed.

> *We must ask if the life we are living is a worthy expression of gratitude for what God has done for us.*

In going on this mission, the soldiers are risking their own lives in order to save a fellow soldier's life. In fact, the mission does claim many lives among the squad sent to save Ryan, including, finally, Captain John Miller, played by Tom Hanks. As he lies mortally wounded, Captain Miller knows that now, finally, Ryan is safe. With his strength fading and his life ebbing away, the captain pulls Ryan down to his face to give him one last command. He looks Ryan in the eyes and says: "Earn this."

Ryan recalls this scene fifty years later, in tears, while visiting the grave of his savior captain. With heartbreaking earnestness and directness he turns to his wife and says, "Tell me I have led a good life. Tell me I'm a good man." He wants to know, in other words, if he has "earned this"—earned the life granted him by the sacrifice of the dead squad members.

Now, as Christians we know that we can never "earn" the life and salvation that the God shown in Christ has given us. We might as well ask if the butterfly has "earned" the beautiful markings on its wings. But we can, we should, we *must* ask if the life we are living is a worthy expression of gratitude for what God has done for us. In other words, we should ask ourselves a question about the shape of our whole lives—our work lives included. We need to address the question not only at the end of our lives but in a continual process of reverifying our life agenda.

When we ask about our "doing," when we consider the use we have made of our will and our energy, our question is not *Have I earned the life I have been given?* but instead, *Has my life been a thankful response to the precious gifts I have been given? Have I,* in short, *worked to spread God's love and lessen the suffering of the world in order to bring God's kingdom more clearly into view?*

When we can answer yes, we will know that we have lived a life of Christian vocation.

QUESTIONS FOR REFLECTION AND DISCUSSION

1. Is your first inclination to see Christianity as all about "being good" or as having nothing to do with being good? Perhaps neither alternative adequately expresses your view, but consider whether you lean in one direction or the other; reflect on why. Then reflect on how you might tell someone new to the faith what Christianity is about.

2. In your heart of hearts, do you think of spending energy as something to rejoice in or as something to avoid? If you habitually find yourself trying to "save" your energy, for what are you saving it? If you often find yourself feeling "spent," do you feel like having run a race well or are you dissipated and distracted from what you truly care about? How might a new understanding of Christian vocation reshape your attitude?

3. Which of Meilaender's four understandings of work (as cocreation; as necessary for leisure; as dignified but irksome; as vocation) characterize your view of your own job or career? How or in what way would one of his categories apply best? Is this predominant view of work shared by your friends and family members? Do you want to continue with this understanding of your career and vocation? Why or why not?

4. If you want to change, in what way would you want your life to be different? Can you think of anyone who has a view of work and vocation more integrated than yours? What specific steps would you have to take to emulate that person?

5. Consider the scene described in *Saving Private Ryan*. In place of Ryan and his wife, imagine that God and you are in conversation. Of course, God will not ask if you have "earned" grace, since no one can earn it. What if, however, God asked, "Has your life shown the gratitude fitting what you have been given?" What would your answer be? Since you are not yet to the point of having that talk face-to-face with God (in other words, you are still alive!), how might you change your attitude and the shape of your life if you anticipate eventually facing that question?

CHAPTER **THREE**

FREEDOM AND OBEDIENCE

THE PARADOX OF "CALLING"
IN THE CHRISTIAN TRADITION

Calling, Freedom, Predestination, and Vocation

When Christians speak about being called, questions about predestination often arise. The scriptures from time to time imply that only some are called, even "predestined," by God.[1] When understood in the wrong way, this concept of predestination can have a devastating effect on motivation for Christian action in the world. In order to develop a powerful and pragmatic view of God's call, then, we cannot avoid thinking about two doctrines that have, unfortunately, often divided Christians—free will and predestination.

Rather than examine these abstractly, let's look at them in the context of real life. After all, our theologizing has to make sense in the midst of the rough contours of lived experience if the gospel is to empower people and change lives. We need to catch a vision of life-as-calling that is both enlivening and realistic. That is, we need to understand our call in a way that makes room for all the types of work Meilaender described. We need an understanding of calling that makes sense of our reality where we sometimes experience work as inherently meaningful and sometimes as irksome. A key theme in the popular film *Forrest Gump* will provide insight.[2]

Freedom and Grace in *Forrest Gump*

The drama of human calling can be found at the heart of the movie *Forrest Gump*. In this film we witness the saga of the world's invitation to an attitude of irony and cynicism and how two people—Forrest and his girlfriend, Jenny—respond to this invitation. In Forrest's life, the dynamics of steadfastness, adherence, and faithfulness face a world that encourages corrupting change and vicious formation. Significantly, Forrest never utters a single sarcastic, or even ironic, word. In contrast, his girlfriend, Jenny, undergoes all the culturally invited transformations available in the late twentieth century, including sexual promiscuity, drug abuse, and a wandering, aimless, Bohemian lifestyle.

Numerous historical events are captured in the film, and the chaotic history of the '50s, '60s, '70s, and '80s builds toward one of the final scenes of the film. In this scene, Forrest, while standing at the grave of his beloved Jenny, tries to make sense of the messiness of lived life—the exultation coupled with the heartbreak, the satisfaction joined with the frustration, the meaning with the absurdity. The question that Forrest Gump poses in the penultimate scene of the movie captures the tense and bewildering reality of life in such a world. Reflecting on the competing philosophies of life represented by two key characters, Forrest says, "I don't know if Mama was right or if it's Lieutenant Dan."

In other words, the options for interpreting life that Forrest had before him were: (1) that we have a fixed destiny—Lieutenant Dan's original philosophy (expressed in his view that he was destined to die in combat, as so many of his family had),[3] or, (2) we are just floating on the apparently random breezes of life's exigencies—in the words of Forrest's

mama, "Life is a box of choco-
lates. . . . You never know what
you're going to get."

At the beginning and at
the end of the film, a floating
feather symbolizes the question
as to which view of life is right.
The feather floats apparently
haphazardly but lands strategi-
cally. Is reality fixed and prede-
termined, or is there some
element of indeterminacy and
room for meaningful under-

> *Conjunctions of human freedom and God's grace do occur, even if at times these transformative conjunctions seem entirely serendipitous.*

standings of human freedom and agency? The answers we
give will greatly affect how we view the possibilities for
human action, the course of human conduct, and our perspective on human work. Our concept of Christian vocation
can become an empty abstraction or an exciting way of life,
depending on our answer to Forrest's question.

The answer to this question is as complex and true to life
as the movement of that feather. Conjunctions of human freedom and God's grace do occur, even if at times these transformative conjunctions seem entirely serendipitous. Life has
undeniably brutal and wounding aspects, many of which seem
to result from the misuse of human freedom. In the film, for
example, Jenny suffered incest at the hands of her father. But
just as undeniably, transforming grace visits us in the midst
of our brokenness, as Forrest's friendship is a recurrent note
of grace in Jenny's life.

> There is a providence; God does provide; God's grace is active.

Finally, I think our answer to Forrest's graveside heart questions about freedom and determinism should be the answer he himself gave. When confronted with the option of adopting either Lieutenant Dan's sense that forces beyond our will ultimately determine our lives or his mama's view that sheer random freedom seems to reign, Gump comes up with his own answer. This man, depicted throughout the film as below average in intelligence and a walking icon of unsophistication, expresses a profoundly sophisticated and powerful view of human life. Forrest says, "I think maybe it's both."

Theologically, we might say that the Christian life holds both a *givenness* and an *openness*. Accepting that helps us understand the paradox of calling in the Christian life: We are called by God, and yet we are free to respond (or not to respond) to that call. And our calling will be lived out in the midst of everybody else's free responses to their callings.

There is a providence; God does provide; God's grace is active. But this providence does not equal "fate" or "destiny" that overrides our freedom. God has given us this freedom to respond to divine grace; we are free to choose. That is why most Christian traditions recognize the possibility of "backsliding" as a real danger. How we use our freedom to respond to God's grace is not a live question only in the minutes before we "make a decision for Christ."

We answer that question continually in the unfolding drama of our lives.

So it is, as Forrest puts it, "both." To put this truth in a related context, we can say that Christians are free *from* sin and also free *for* obedience, not just one or the other. We must embrace both understandings of freedom if we are to live out our vocations as Christians. As 2 Timothy 1:6 says, we are to "fan into flame the gift of God" (NIV). God plants a burning desire to lead a life for God, but we are the ones who are responsible for "fanning the flame."

But how do we deal with such a messy and confusing conglomeration of freedom and determination? How can we start to sort out what we can do and what we can't? One important step will be to name some of the limitations of human freedom recognized in the Christian view.

THREE LIMITATIONS ON HUMAN FREEDOM

Many realities of human life affect how we view both God's activity in the world and the possible scope for our human responses. Let us look at three limiting features of human life.

Finitude

Being finite simply means not being infinite. We are "creatures." As the root of this word implies, we are *created*. We are not self-sufficient. We have a beginning, caused when God called us into being. God is our Creator. This means, as the opposite of *infinite* implies, we have limits. We are not in charge of all reality; we are but a part of the larger created reality.

> *True Christian humility means that compared to God, we are not all that much.*

The fact of our finitude has numerous implications, but perhaps most significantly it calls us to *humility*. Humility does not mean denying how precious we are in God's eyes, which is false humility. True Christian humility means that compared to God, we are not all that much (see Ps. 8:3-6: "What are human beings that you are mindful of them?").

But, to guard us from going too far with an incorrect concept of humility, we must also appreciate that we are "fearfully and wonderfully made" (Ps. 139:14). We are created in the image of God (Gen. 1:26-27). We are beings redeemed by the death of the Son of God (John 3:16). In short, we are, in God's eyes, precious.

Knowing that we don't have to puff ourselves up and pretend to be something we are not provides a powerful and exciting glimpse of our true freedom. God does not expect us masterfully to manipulate all of life. God just expects us to be faithful wherever we are. In short, God does not expect what finite beings cannot accomplish. God loves our finite creatureliness, and God calls us to be about only what finite creatures can do.

One of the most important truths implied in our finitude is that God will one day call us to death. God created us as finite—mortal. The Genesis story tells us that we were not originally created to be eternal. God drove Adam and Eve from the

Garden in part because if they had stayed, they might have eaten of the tree of life and lived forever. They were created with the potential to be eternal but were not in fact eternal (see Gen. 3:22-23). As the author of Ecclesiastes puts it, there will be, for all of us, "a time to die" (3:2). We all owe God a death, and there will be no welshing on that debt!

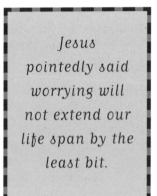

Jesus pointedly said worrying will not extend our life span by the least bit.

Realizing our limited and finite nature sometimes seems to paralyze human activity and cancel out any meaning or purpose to life, but this truth can, instead, give meaning to life. If we only have so many days on earth, then we should, like the inmates in the movie *The Shawshank Redemption*, see that this leaves us only two options: "Get busy living or get busy dying." We Christians have died one death already at our baptism—we all are baptized into the death of Christ (Rom. 6:3)—so we are now free to "get busy living." Yes, we all will die, but now death has lost its sting (1 Cor. 15:55-56). We need not fear that death will cancel out the meaning of our lives.

Jesus pointedly said worrying will not extend our life span by the least bit (Luke 12:25), so we should neither ignore our limited nature nor let it dominate our lives. Accepting our finitude is not the death of our freedom. It is its birth.

Sin

> *We are called to a life of hope, and not despair, because God has dealt with sin.*

Our finitude imposes a limited scope on our freedom. Another limitation relates to what Christians refer to as sin.

It is possible to misuse our God-given freedom. In fact, we do it all the time. Christianity calls the misuse of our freedom an act of sin. Uncountable instances of humans misusing freedom fill the past. Sometimes the cumulative effect of all this misuse of freedom—by ourselves and others—leaves us very few options with which to exercise our human freedom. At any one time we are not as free as we might have been if we lived in a sin-free world.

In faith, though, we trust God's grace to inhabit even the most limited set of options, making possible God's redemptive purposes. Recognizing the widespread nature of sin and acknowledging that this can hinder the use of our freedom should not lead us to despair, just as realizing our finitude should not. We are called to a life of hope, and not despair, because God has dealt with sin.

God's forgiveness of sin through the work of Christ on the cross has freed us from the power and guilt of sin. We need not submerge our own sins in our consciousness; they should be confessed. Any informed order of communal worship, any well-rounded liturgy, calls for such confession. When we confess our sinfulness, we are freed from the power and guilt of our sins and are free to use the energy

God has given us to do God's will in the world.

Still the consequences of human sin must be dealt with in the world. These consequences can significantly affect how we can use our freedom. If I misuse my freedom by driving drunk and kill someone, God will forgive that misuse of my freedom if I honestly confess it and truly repent, but the person killed will still be dead. My drunk driving—my misuse of my freedom—my sin—will materially affect how all involved in that event can use their freedom in the future. While we can say with assurance that God's will cannot finally be thwarted by human sinfulness, how we use and misuse our freedom can and does affect the possible options for the future use of our freedom.

> *Once again the true nature of our freedom is revealed when we name and claim who we are in God's sight.*

When we confess our sinfulness, however, and seek afresh God's guiding presence in our lives, we can see that God creates new possibilities for human flourishing. Perhaps paradoxically, claiming and acknowledging the limiting nature of our sinfulness does not limit our freedom. Once again the true nature of our freedom is revealed when we name and claim who we are in God's sight. Just as seeing our finitude does not keep us from living out our call but instead allows us to discern our call more fully, recognizing our sinfulness can illuminate the best path that leads us home.

Brokenness

Our finitude calls for humility and shows the appropriate scope of our freedom. Our sinfulness calls for confession, repentance, and forgiveness and reminds us that our freedom can go dreadfully wrong if we listen to our own selfish voice instead of heeding God's call. But what happens when other people's misuse of their freedom affects us? When someone abuses us? When someone unjustly fires us? When we are hurt in an accident we didn't cause? At such times we experience brokenness. Brokenness does not, in its essence, call for deepening our humility, as finitude does; nor does it call for acts of repentance and forgiveness, as our sinfulness does. Brokenness calls for healing.

Our need for healing shows our continual dependence on God's grace in a world of misused freedom. And God's grace *is* there for us. We must never think of our freedom as if we were set adrift to manage life completely on our own. God is with us! (See Matt. 28:20.) God's Holy Spirit can help us overcome even the misuse of freedom by others. And, again, when we call out for healing from the misuse of freedom by others, the limited but real nature of our freedom comes into sharper focus. It is a freedom of constant dependence. God will give us the resources we need for any spiritual challenge, but we must use our freedom to acknowledge our dependence and ask God into our brokenness.

Knowing the reality of our finitude, our sinfulness, and our brokenness reveals the truly complex landscape in which we live out our calling. It becomes clear that not every obstacle, stumbling block, or blind alley arises from God's direct action. Conversely, while we should reserve our truest praise for only God, our own free human cooperation with God's Spirit can help to bring about real, palpable good in God's creation, and our role in God's economy must be acknowledged. Living a life of real, not pretend, freedom means life will never be completely predictable. Human freedom and both its possibilities and real limitations bend and shape this world in almost unimaginable ways.

In the midst of this confusing turmoil, remember that God created the world full of limited beings, capable of sin and capable of being hurt—all using and misusing their freedom on a daily basis. If we totally rebel against these harsh and confusing realities by rejecting or being indifferent to God and God's creation, we rebel against the God who put us here. Even though we live in a world where God's will coexists with the limitations of finitude, sinfulness, and brokenness, we cannot simply close our ears to God's call for action. God calls us into God's creation to help set creation right, to use our limited, sinful, and broken freedom to bring about a better incarnation of God's kingdom on earth.

Limitations on Freedom and Different Understandings of Work

Adopting this point of view—that we are both free and limited, that our freedom is simultaneously God-given, God-limited, and humanly deformed—will allow us to accept an understanding of work worthy of our call. The exigencies and contingencies that arise in our attempts to live out our

> When we do not get the job of our dreams, we cannot give up on our calling or become cynical about the very concept.

calling in the world of work should not necessarily be seen as God's direct interventions in our lives. When we do not get the job of our dreams, the one we think we are "called" to, or when we are laid off from our dream job, or when a sexist or racist boss keeps us from living out our potential, we cannot give up on our calling or become cynical about the very concept. We can never allow the worldly mockers to interpret our failures and hardships for us through their jaded filters and conclude that anyone who follows a call is foolishly deluded. It is never a choice between having a calling and encountering failure and frustration. As Forrest Gump noted, "It's both."

We cannot allow our halting and often-failed attempts to realize the exalted understandings of work—work as cocreation and work as vocation—to cast a pall of meaninglessness over our everyday energy expenditures. Given the reality of human freedom and its limitations, the results of our energy expenditures will only occasionally be obvious as an explicit example of work called forth by God. We do need to embrace a view of work as potentially cocreation and as our vocation. But since we live in this mixed world of good creation and fallen sinfulness (a world described in Genesis 1 and 3)—a world where people are free to refuse to acknowledge their finitude, sinfulness, and brokenness—sometimes work will be simply irksome, and at times we will see it only as a means to achieving leisure. If we are faithful, though, we will find God already working in the midst of our confusing world, calling us to join in God's work.

As we take up this call, we must continually remind ourselves that how we make our living in this free, sinful, and broken world is *not* the same as our calling. A career can be consistent with our calling, and at times the way we make a living can be an expression of our calling. But, simply put, our job is not our calling. So just how might we explain in some detail what our calling can look like in the real world? To this we turn next.

QUESTIONS FOR REFLECTION AND DISCUSSION

1. What reaction do you have when topics like freedom, destiny, and predestination arise in discussions? Does the idea of predestination give you a sense of comfort because "God is in control," or does it dispirit you because all human effort seems useless? Does the idea of a sovereign God imply that in a literal way God must control and will everything that happens?

2. Does the idea that humans are free scare you or enliven you? Is it possible to allow both feelings to coexist in your heart and mind without having to suppress or drive out one or the other? If God is the Creator of all that is and humans are created in God's image, can you imagine freedom as part of that image? Many people feel most alive when they are creative. How does freedom affect creativity?

3. We face finitude in many aspects of life. We do not have unlimited power, wisdom, or knowledge, to name just a few areas where our finitude is evident. We tend to resist awareness that we all will die one day. Is it possible for you to acknowledge and claim that truth without being morbid or depressed? Consider the Christian adage that only what we do for God will last beyond our death. How might that thought influence your view of Christian vocation?

4. How has sin—the misuse of freedom, both by others and by ourselves—limited your own expression of freedom? Can you name particular examples? How could understanding these sinful acts as forgiven affect their impact on human freedom? Consider the same questions regarding human brokenness, that is, when someone else's misuse of freedom negatively affects you. Can you give specific examples that show how our own brokenness can limit freedom, both our own and that of others? Be specific about particular instances and especially about how God's healing of our brokenness can open up new paths for using our freedom.

CHAPTER **FOUR**

LIVING AND WORKING
FROM THE HEART

Spiritual but Not Religious?

We are called to God, to be God's, to live for God, to work for God's purposes—and, finally, to help realize God's kingdom on earth as it is in heaven. God, through the activity of the Holy Spirit, makes it possible for us to choose to work with God in finite, sinful, and broken creation. What does that mean in practical terms? What does it look like to be a Christian in today's world?

"I'm not religious, but I am spiritual." We often hear this refrain today. It's somewhat parallel to Rick's claim in *Casablanca* that he is no good at being noble. Who wants to be seen as religious, especially if people think that's all about "being good," as discussed in chapter 2? Anyone self-identifying as religious stands in danger of that deplorable, moralistic label "Goody Two-shoes." If that is the case, we can appreciate why people would disavow the claim to be religious.

But just what do people mean when they say they are "spiritual but not religious"? Answers may vary widely, but from my observations, people who make such a statement seem to have one characteristic in common: they hold deep feelings and commitments. They claim that rather than merely parroting conventional wisdom about stereotypical religious values, they have appropriated and are profoundly committed to certain deep truths confirmed experientially.

If that hypothesis applies to at least some such folks, a problem becomes apparent. According to this understanding, being "spiritual" means little more than saying, "I am sincere about certain commitments." This is problematic because being sincere by itself does not establish the value of whatever people are sincere about.

Consider a parallel taken from a popular country song. In "Not That Different," Collin Raye sings about having a lot in common with a girl—they are really "not that different"—and therefore should become a couple, because he laughs, loves, hopes, tries, hurts, needs, fears, and cries. Since he knows she does too, they are "really not that different."[1]

We can grant that these common capacities do establish minimal, human commonalities, but the most interesting questions about human identity are not answered by such assertions. The truly interesting questions come next: About *what* do you laugh? Over *what* do you cry? What is the *source* of your hope? *What* or *whom* do you love, and *why*?

The fact that we all have the capacity for sincere human emotion does not mean that we govern or express those emotions in the same way. Only when we know the values, commitments, and beliefs that form people's emotions—the grammar of the heart—can we recognize their essence or center. From a Christian perspective, the mere fact that individuals have capacity for emotions within them tells us very little about their "spirituality."

Christians cannot settle for such a minimalistic description of spiritual life. As Christians, we are focused on following a particular calling. We are provided an agenda for spiritual and emotional maturity—a grammar by which we should shape our hearts, a grammar that tells us how to be—

and do. Let's describe that grammar by beginning with what we already have claimed as central to our Christian vocation: our call to live in—and to further—God's kingdom.

WHAT IT MEANS TO LIVE IN THE KINGDOM OF GOD

Living as if God is our King means being in a relationship in which God is the sovereign, the One who has ultimate sway over us, the One who has the final say. To understand this, think about a recognizable human parallel. To live properly as a citizen of England is to live as if the queen is your sovereign. One's life is marked by obedience to Her Majesty's laws. It is possible to live in the realm of England physically and yet not live as if the queen is your sovereign, for example, by paying no attention to the laws of the land.

The same stands true for the kingdom of God. We all live in God's world, and in that sense we all are God's creatures. But not all of us live as if God were our sovereign, typically because we have difficulty dealing with our finitude, sinfulness, and brokenness. For this reason, we often find ourselves *not* living the lives for which God's creatures were made. In short, we are living contrary to God's law.

But how should Christians understand God's law? Some interpret God's law in a moralistic way as a long list of dos and dont's. Those who take this approach tend to see the Christian life as primarily about being good. Relating to God through a list of dos and dont's is what Paul, in his many New Testament writings, ruled out. However, Jesus said

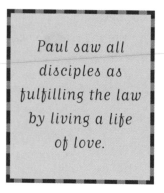

Paul saw all disciples as fulfilling the law by living a life of love.

he came not to abolish the law but to fulfill it (Matt. 5:17), and Paul saw all disciples as fulfilling the law by living a life of love (Rom. 13:10). To act with love as the motivation for all that you do is to live by the law. To lead a life of love is to live in God's kingdom, to live in recognition that God is sovereign.

Love, however, can take on many forms and be expressed in many ways. We can distinguish Christian love more clearly by studying a scripture passage that describes what God's Spirit looks like when it is fully expressed in the world.

CALLED TO LIVE FROM THE HEART

Toward the end of his letter to the Galatians, Paul describes the two main competing ways of life that Christians have before them. According to Paul, one way of life is marked by the "works of the flesh"; the other, by the "fruit of the Spirit." In explaining the best use of our free will, Paul lists what Christians are to be free *from* as well as what they are to be free *for*. His words show us that living as a citizen in the kingdom of God is not like living under the law of a kingdom as we normally think about it. Living as if God is our sovereign entails living under the guidance of the Holy Spirit:

> You were called to freedom, brothers and sisters;
> only do not use your freedom as an opportunity for
> self-indulgence, but through love become slaves to
> one another. For the whole law is summed up in a
> single commandment, "You shall love your neigh-
> bor as yourself." If, however, you bite and devour
> one another, take care that you are not consumed
> by one another.
>
> Live by the Spirit, I say, and do not gratify the
> desires of the flesh. For what the flesh desires is
> opposed to the Spirit, and what the Spirit desires is
> opposed to the flesh; for these are opposed to each
> other, to prevent you from doing what you want.
> But if you are led by the Spirit, you are not subject
> to the law. Now the works of the flesh are obvious:
> fornication, impurity, licentiousness, idolatry, sor-
> cery, enmities, strife, jealousy, anger, quarrels, dis-
> sensions, factions, envy, drunkenness, carousing,
> and things like these. I am warning you, as I warned
> you before: those who do such things will not inherit
> the kingdom of God. (Gal. 5:13-21)

When Paul denigrates the "works of the flesh," he is not
saying that our bodies are bad and our "spirits" are good.
"Flesh" for Paul is shorthand for an entire way of life that
ignores God's Spirit, tries to exist without God, does not
acknowledge God as sovereign. This life, operating as if
"flesh" is all there is, stands in opposition to the life of the
Spirit. This Spirit-led life, Paul goes on to say, can be compared to a fruit tree. If a tree grows certain fruit, you can
bet that it is a certain kind of tree. So it is with the life of
the Spirit.

> By contrast [to the works of the flesh], the fruit of
> the Spirit is love, joy, peace, patience, kindness, gen-
> erosity, faithfulness, gentleness, and self-control.
> There is no law against such things. And those who
> belong to Christ Jesus have crucified the flesh with
> its passions and desires. If we live by the Spirit, let
> us also be guided by the Spirit. Let us not become
> conceited, competing against one another, envying
> one another. (Gal. 5:22-26)

The alternative way of life to the works of the flesh is living the "fruit of the Spirit." When the Holy Spirit is growing
within you, your life will show these fruit as an apple tree
shows its true nature by growing apples. Living by the Spirit
radically shapes living out a life of Christian vocation.

To live as God has called us to live most fundamentally
means leading a life marked by certain character traits. God
is our sovereign when our lives are marked by love, joy,
peace, patience, kindness, generosity, faithfulness, gentleness,
and self-control. Our calling, our vocation, is to lead such a
life marked by the fruit of the Spirit. Nothing more and nothing less. Seeing the fruit of the Spirit in this way suggests a
connection between these fruit and another measure of
human excellence—the virtues.

Virtues are capacities that help achieve some end. The
ability to drive a nail quickly, straight, and true is a virtue
for a carpenter, as is the ability to cut a straight line in wood.
A person with enough of such virtuous capacities can be a
good carpenter. To appreciate the virtues of the Christian
life, we need to look at them in relation to the end or goal

that they help to achieve. The kingdom of God is that end, that goal, that orienting concern.

When our lives are unmistakably marked by these attributes, whether we call them fruits or virtues, we relate correctly to God, and we have a foretaste of the kingdom of God—an experience of heaven on earth.

LIVING THE FRUIT OF THE SPIRIT

Recently many good studies have explored living the fruit of the Spirit, and I do not need to try to replicate this fine work.[2] However, I want to address a couple of common misconceptions about this life of the Spirit manifested in these fruit.

First of all, living a life that bears these fruit does not suggest constantly *feeling* them. A person can perform a loving act without feeling love at the time. When a mother with stomach flu drags herself out of bed to change a wailing baby's diaper, sensations of love probably never enter that scenario, but a loving act is accomplished nonetheless. Without denying that episodes of strong feeling occur, it is crucial to recognize that the fruit of the Spirit are more like dispositions to behave in certain ways than intense sensations.[3]

Secondly, though human beings exhibit a tremendous variety of what we call temperaments or personalities, living the "fruit of the Spirit" is not optional depending on our score on the Myers-Briggs test or any other scheme for categorizing humanity. We cannot say, for instance, that it is fine for Juanita to be joyful because that is her temperament, but Sven naturally acts sullen, so we should just accept his behavior. We cannot say—as Christians—that it's okay for Jerry to be impatient because he is very demanding and does not suffer fools gladly; he is just that type of guy.

Variations among people exist; we respect and honor them. But love, joy, peace, and the rest of the fruit are not capacities like being double-jointed, which individuals are born with or without. Through the power of the Holy Spirit, people can and do become more loving, joyful, patient, and so on. We call this process growing in grace, becoming mature, and, in theological language, growing in "sanctification" or holiness. Allowing for different "natural" tendencies and endowments does not rule out the possibility of change. When people call something second nature, they suggest it did not come "naturally" (according to their "first nature") but that, over time, through practice and encouragement that tendency or skill has become a part of who they are—"second nature." Acknowledging, as part of the mystery of creation, that we all start at different places in the process of growing these various fruit does not rule out the potential for all to make progress.

Making progress requires having a goal, and this list of fruit provides the goal of our spiritual life on earth. Having a specific exemplar of these fruit can furnish a concrete guide for our lives. That is why studying the lives of saints (either literally or figuratively speaking) can help us grow. We may never achieve the level of compassion that Mother Teresa exhibited, but looking at her life inspires compassion in us.

EMOTION, REASON, AND MEN

It might be beneficial to reflect on gender roles and emotion. Let's face it: the fruit of the Spirit are, to a large extent, emotional capacities. Men—especially those of Northern European descent in contemporary Western society—regard most emotions as the enemy. Typically the male party line claims emotions "get in the way" and "cloud judgment." "Reason" is the goal, whether in the business culture of efficient management where practical reason rules or the scientific arena that produces truth worthy of being quoted in the newspapers. Perhaps this explains the power in the country song lyric mentioned earlier: it just might come as a revelation to some women that, in fact, men do cry!

Of course, this myth of "reason" has come under assault from many directions in the academic world. Those familiar with so-called postmodern thinking will know that the Enlightenment ideal of a universally accessible, unequivocal reason that can discern all truth claims has come in for serious criticism by male as well as female scholars.[4] Other contemporary philosophers, with no such large-scale postmodern ideological ax to wield, have studied the nature of emotion and found that the often-assumed "split" between reason and emotion does not stand up to scrutiny.[5]

Aside from these intellectual wars of academia, though, another observation raises doubt about the supposed male elevation of reason over emotion. The fact is men do endorse emotions but usually only certain ones. Anger and lust come to mind as typical deviations from reason that men allow if not always endorse or encourage. Watching a football game, then, is a good example of a permissible emotional outlet for men.

Football is a violent game, played by men who are trained to be, as many a coach has said, "agile and mobile and hostile." The prototypical male fan is invited to get passionately attached to his team and vicariously participate in the victory (or loss). When the violence and ritualized anger of the action on the field are punctuated by shots of the cheerleaders and dance teams—as well as the bumping and grinding of the halftime shows—we have a perfect cocktail of allowable male emotion—anger and lust. It should be no surprise, then, that Super Bowl Sunday is an especially exciting and meaningful day for many men.

Men need to recognize that emotion already plays a part in their lives. The question for men becomes the one Paul posed: *Which* emotions do you want to mark your heart? Emotions are not some dispensable luxury like flowers in a window box. Love, joy, and peace are the very stuff of life. Not only that, but being a Christian includes having our emotions formed in a particular way, having strong emotions for the right reasons.

THE RIGHT FRUIT FOR THE RIGHT REASON

If we love, for example, because we think it will benefit us in our social relations or in getting something for ourselves, we will not have a love that "endures all things" (1 Cor. 13:7). That kind of manipulative love usually vanishes at the first sign of adversity. Similarly, if we take joy in our stock portfolio or our prestigious job, our joy will leave when the market dips and our company goes under. If our peace depends on what the newscast reports, if our patience lasts as long as it's not too costly, we will not be living the fruit of the Spirit.

God's Spirit calls us to love because God first loved us (I John 4:19), to take joy in our salvation and in the joy of others (see I Pet. 1:8-9), to be at peace because we have been reconciled to God (John 16:33 and Acts 10:36). These connections between the gospel and the emotions of our heart are what we might call the grammar of our faith, which becomes the grammar of our heart.

This emphasis on the life of the heart does not take away from the power of practical reason in managing a company or the explanatory power of the scientific method in finding cures for diseases. It does, however, show that such an instrumental focus of our reasoning powers does not encompass the full human story. When properly understood, practical and scientific reasoning ultimately should find their highest use in the service of growing the fruit of the Spirit.

Yes, the fruit come from the Spirit and cannot be created by human effort. But like actual fruit, the yield can be greatly increased by pruning, watering, and fertilizing—all activities that the faithful steward of the trees can undertake. Anyone who thinks growing worthwhile fruit is a passive business needs to have a serious talk with a farmer about the realities of agriculture!

In growing these fruit, first we must discern prayerfully if our current lives are marked more by works of the

Love implies being concerned with others!

flesh or fruit of the Spirit. In other words, we must start with a clear and humble self-knowledge. In light of our analysis and guided by the Spirit, we then start pruning the works of the flesh and fertilizing the Spirit in our heart. If we are accustomed to getting energy from anger, we will need to envision instead a life motivated by love. If lust determines personal interaction, we must learn how to care for another without self-interest as the driving force. Cultivating the fruit of the Spirit in this way and growing them for the right reasons will motivate our most sustained and focused energy expenditures. In short, it should be our deepest and truest vocation. A life marked by the fruit of the Spirit is a comprehensive response to human suffering, brokenness, finitude, and sin. It is a way to recognize God as sovereign.

Does the goal of growing the fruit of the Spirit entail a life of introspection and self-concern? No, because all the fruit of the Spirit concern relationships, and other people are best situated to tell us whether love, joy, peace, and so forth mark our relationships. Taking love as our goal does not imply primary concern with our own spiritual temperatures; instead, love implies being concerned with others!

HOW DOES THIS HAPPEN?

It is crucial, then, to ask *how* we catch a vision of living a life motivated by love, *how* to fix our peace on unshakable ground, *how* to become patient in a hectic world, *how* to be self-controlled in the face of the centrifugal forces of our culture. Believe it or not, the church exists on earth to address these very questions.

"What!" you might say. "You mean that messy collection of finite, sinful, and broken people that meets once a week in a building constantly in need of maintenance? I should hang out with those folks in order to grow the fruit of the Spirit?"

Yes.

A well-ordered worship service even—or especially— in the midst of finite, sinful, and broken people, will help to grow God's fruit. Worship's nurturing elements include hearing the story of God's action through Bible reading and preaching, praying, and participating in those special instruments of God's Spirit, the sacraments of baptism and Communion.

To illustrate the transforming effect of the sacraments, let me once again look to a film. Without denigrating the importance of baptism (which should not be overlooked),[6] I want to focus here on the sacrament meant to be available throughout a believer's life, the Lord's Supper, or the Eucharist.

A MEAL THAT CHANGES THINGS: *BABETTE'S FEAST*

Many readers will not be as familiar with *Babette's Feast* as with *Casablanca* or *Forrest Gump*, but it is a powerful film that won an Academy Award for Best Foreign Language Film for 1988. Set in nineteenth-century Denmark, it tells the story of two sisters, but it also tells the story of human transformation and Christian vocation.

The sisters are daughters of a religious leader whose strict piety draws a small but dedicated following. The daughters believe their place in life is to support their father's ministry. Accordingly, one daughter, blessed with a beautiful singing voice, turns her back on a lucrative opera career in order to stay and sing hymns with her village. The other daughter likewise says no to the allures of the world in the form of a handsome army officer who courts her. She stays in the village, remains single, and, with her sister, grows old trying to hold together the increasingly cantankerous congregation of followers of their now-deceased father.

Into their lives comes a poor French woman seeking shelter from the chaos of revolution in her home country. The sisters cannot afford to hire her, but she desires only to stay with them and take care of their household in exchange for food and lodging. The sisters take her in. This is Babette.

Babette lives for many years with the sisters, and she proves to be a great asset to them. She is an efficient manager of the house, and she eventually learns to make the humble peasant food that has sustained the sisters all of their lives. Then something happens.

Babette had a friend in France who would buy her a lottery ticket every time the lottery was held. One day, Babette learns that she has won ten thousand francs—a sum almost too large for this humble household to comprehend. The sisters know that this windfall will facilitate Babette's escape from simple servitude, and it undoubtedly will precipitate her return to France; they mourn this loss. Babette asks one final favor. She wants permission to serve the sisters and the remnants of their father's congregation a French meal—a celebration meal held in honor of the departed father's birthday.

The sisters reluctantly agree, but they have no idea what they are in for. Babette orders in all sorts of strange food for this special occasion, including many items never before seen by the pious sisters. The resulting meal is truly a feast, served on the finest china and featuring turtle soup, quail, fancy breads, desserts, and an endless stream of exotic wines and liqueurs. The most striking thing about this feast, though, is its effect on the invited congregation.

As the film depicted them, the people had, over the years, become quarrelsome and bitter, angry and closed in on themselves, full of remorse, regret, and unhealed animosities over slights and injustices from previous decades. Their "worship services" were anything but. As these individuals work their way through Babette's feast, however, a change evolves.

Before the meal, the guests promise one another that they will not comment on the food as a way of showing that they are spiritual people—unaffected by things of this world. "It will be as if we never had the sense of taste," they promise. But as they consume the food, they cannot keep themselves from enjoying it, and they start feeling the results of its sensual delights.

The dinner guests begin letting go of their petty jealousies and their soul-twisting angers. Words of confession, repentance, and forgiveness are spoken to one another. In the end, they join hands in a circle outside and sing one of the preacher's hymns. As they depart, one sister comments that the stars seem closer to earth that night.

In this meal and its effects, we catch a cinematic glimpse of what Communion can be—a meal that changes people, a meal that makes a difference. In glimpsing the rich possibilities of life available through the exquisite food and drink, the people catch a glimpse of a reality beyond what they thought possible. They not only catch a glimpse of a new way of life, they start to live it. The stars have come closer. Heaven has touched the earth. The life of the Spirit is possible not just after death in heaven but here on earth as well.

The church has understood Communion in a similar way. The liturgy for this sacrament reflects this sense. Perhaps if we took the time to think about, and pray about, these words, our experience of Communion could resemble what Babette's feast engendered in those Danish villagers. A traditional prayer before Communion conveys what the believer looks for in this meal that makes a difference. Perhaps that will whet your appetite for this feast—a meal that is all about growing the fruit of the Spirit.

> Grant us . . . , gracious Lord,
>> so to partake of this Sacrament of thy Son Jesus Christ,
>> that we may walk in newness of life,
>> may grow into his likeness,
>> and may evermore dwell in him, and he in us. Amen.[7]

Babette and Christian Vocation

After Babette's feast has been consumed, Babette cleans up, and the sisters come and speak to her about her imminent departure. They are stunned by what Babette then reveals to them. The feast has cost her entire winnings. She has no money left and will stay as their cook and housekeeper.

How can this be? Why would she spend all her money setting a feast before those who could not—would not—appreciate it? Babette then tells the sisters that in France she was a highly honored—even revered—chef. In the words of one of her admirers, she was a cook who could transform a dinner into a love affair—"a love affair that made no distinction between bodily appetite and spiritual appetite." She was forced to give up her art to serve as a humble cook preparing rough peasant food of dried cod and bread. This feast offered a chance to show her appreciation for what the sisters had done by taking her in. But it was more than that.

After revealing the truth about the meal, Babette, standing tall and proud, says that an artist asks only one thing: "Give me the chance to do my very best."

Just as Christ gave his all on the cross so that we might eat the meal of salvation, so Babette gave her all for the transforming meal.

In the juxtaposition of the sisters and Babette, we see contrasting visions of Christian vocation. The sisters considered denying the joys of this world their expression of faith—giving up a singing career and eschewing the married life. Babette, expressing the worldly skills of a premier chef through her extravagant meal, showed the sisters another way.

Using talents she had been given as well as skills honed in years of work, Babette was able to show the congregation that earth and heaven can touch. In the oft-quoted words of their father, "righteousness and bliss can kiss." Here is a vision of the kingdom where "righteousness"—that religious word for right-relatedness—can kiss "bliss"—that secular word for extreme physical pleasure. Even the sisters, who lived with wonderings, if not regret, about the lives to which they said no, are reconciled with their pasts through Babette's outpouring of love.[8]

While singing with a voice coach traveling through their town, the sister with a beautiful voice had sung a passage from Mozart. The words she repeated in the song can be no coincidence; they speak directly to the theme of the film. "I'm fearful of my joy," she sang, and she and her sister seemingly were afraid of their joy. They thought Christian joy could come only through denying God-given gifts evident in their lives.

We are called to take up our crosses and follow Christ (Matt. 16:24), and there will be seasons when not exercising all our gifts will be the right course of action. But it is a perversion of Christian calling to think that God wants us to renounce the very gifts given us and not use them in ways that glorify God.

"Righteousness and bliss can kiss." These words from the father's sermon found expression in Babette's life. God created our heart, and it is God's plan that we have our heart's desire. As Jesus said, "I came that they may have life, and have it abundantly" (John 10:10). We will be thankful if, like Babette, we taste—even fleetingly—the marriage of bliss and righteousness.

QUESTIONS FOR REFLECTION AND DISCUSSION

1. Have you ever encountered anyone who said—or have you ever said—"I am not religious, but I am spiritual"? How do you understand that distinction? Is being spiritual related to emotions and motivations characteristic of an individual? How else do you understand what it means to be spiritual?

2. What emotions would you say typically characterize you? Are any of them among the "works of the flesh" or the "fruit of the spirit"? Would other people name the same emotions in describing you? If the "real you" is not apparent to people, what can you change to make the appearance match the reality?

3. When you hear the phrase "the kingdom of God," what comes into your mind? Is it "heaven," understood as the reality that Christians are to experience after life on earth? Why do you think Jesus taught his disciples to pray for "God's kingdom" to come to earth and for God's will to be done on earth "as it is in heaven"? Do we understand this language exclusively in an apocalyptic way, or is it possible that we are called to be God's tools for helping to spread the realm of God further *on earth*?

4. Have you seen the sacraments serve as a bridge between God and humanity? If so, how? when? If not, how might this possibility create new understandings

of transformative human action in your world? In what way can the incarnation of Christ serve as a model for human action in the world, a model for living out our vocation?

5. Entertain the possibility that someone could grant you the ability to have absolutely any kind of life you would want. What words would you use to describe that life? Would it primarily be a life of "pleasure," or would concepts like "happiness" or "joy" be more prominent? Try listing specific acts that would mark such a life. Now compare them to the "works of the flesh" and the "fruit of the Spirit" and consider how these acts might be classified.

6. What would it take for "righteousness" and "bliss" to kiss each other in your life? How might these terms be fleshed out and lived? Would a focus on others rather than fulfillment of all our passions characterize such a life, perhaps even be the primary focus? How would that focus require swimming against the tide of our culture?

CHAPTER FIVE

FULFILLMENT IN VOCATION

A CHRISTIAN VISION

TRYING TO CATCH A VISION

Immanuel Kant, influential nineteenth-century German philosopher, in his *Lectures on Ethics*, says:

> There are two methods by which [people] arrive at an opinion of their worth: by comparing themselves with the idea of perfection and by comparing themselves with others. The first of these methods is sound; the second is not, and it frequently even leads to a result diametrically opposed to the first.[1]

Even though he seems to reject entirely comparing ourselves to others, Kant goes on to hold out some redeeming possibilities for this approach. Kant says the jealousy that inevitably comes from comparing ourselves to one who is superior can lead in one of two directions, one more pathological and the other more helpful.

> When a man compares himself with another and finds that the other has many more good points, he becomes jealous of each and every good point he discovers in the other, and tries to depreciate it so that his own good points may stand out. This kind of jealousy may be called grudging. The other species of the genus jealousy, which makes us try to add to our good points so as to compare well with another, may be called emulating jealousy. The jealousy of emulation is, as we have stated, more difficult than

the jealousy of grudge and so is much the less fre-
quent of the two.[2]

Rather than try to discern the best way to live out our
vocation by comparing our calling to an abstract ideal, we
might do what Kant called a dangerous but occasionally useful undertaking: compare ourselves to others. I want to recognize the wisdom of Kant's analysis by lifting up both a
negative example of what can happen when we compare our
calling to that of others and a more positive example.

THE NEED TO MIND OUR OWN CALL

We cannot determine the setting, job, or circumstance that
best expresses our calling at any one time solely by observ-
ing how others live their callings. Judging our calling by comparing it to anyone else's can lead to what Kant called
grudging jealousy. It also could be called envy, one of the
works of the flesh we are to avoid. Such jealousy can also
be described as coveting, specifically prohibited in the tenth
commandment. This kind of jealousy leads, in the extreme,
to a life of destructive rebellion against God. We put ourselves in God's place, telling God what gifts, talents, and
opportunities we should have been given; we become filled
with venom toward anyone who has what we desire.

Anyone familiar with the scriptures can acknowledge
that this attitude is forbidden; describing the behavior and
its effects in the real world is more difficult. Again the arts
can aid our perception of these truths. In the film *Amadeus*
we find a vivid illustration of grudging jealousy or envy.

The main character and narrator, Antonio Salieri, a highly honored eighteenth-century composer, held a privileged position at the court of the emperor. The problem was that Salieri happened to be living at the same time as perhaps the greatest composer of symphonic music, Wolfgang Amadeus Mozart. Hearing the beauty and majesty that Mozart was able to express made Salieri's own talent seem paltry by comparison. The comparison's effect devastated Salieri's life.

> *When it comes to vocation, we can and should emulate good examples and take them as an inspiration.*

In one of the film's most dramatic scenes, Salieri's realization of Mozart's surpassing gift of talent and art leads him to turn his back on God. As he deliberately places his crucifix into a fire, he vows that from that day forward he will be God's enemy. He will work to block and frustrate the talents he has glimpsed in the incomparable Mozart.

Salieri was gifted and spent much of his life using his gift to God's glory. But he fell into this tragic error of forming a sense of himself and his career by comparison with someone else's expression of God's calling. When it comes to vocation, we can and should emulate good examples and take them as an inspiration. But deriving our own sense of worth by hating or trying to destroy superior examples God has put in this world will do nothing but lead us away from our true calling to love God and our neighbor. Paul concludes the "fruit of the Spirit" passage with the admonition "Let us not become conceited, competing against one another, envying one another" (Gal. 5:26).

ADMIRATION AND THE POWER OF HOLY EXAMPLES

Kant saw, though, that jealousy need not always lead to such destructive ends. Jealousy, rightly understood, can serve ennobling ends. This is what Kant called "emulating jealousy"; we might call it admiration. Roman Catholics study the lives of the saints in order to benefit from the positive, transformative examples of others. For the same reason, John Wesley published biographies of exemplary Christians in his *Arminian Magazine*.

Here I would like to offer Thomas à Becket as an example that Christians today might emulate when trying to discern their vocational path. We'll look at his life as depicted in the film *Becket*. In order to make sense of the film and Becket's life, however, we must reacquaint ourselves with a term popular in the Middle Ages, a term often used in assessing a life as a whole: *honor.*

Often *honor* has been understood to be a quality individuals either do or do not have based on their dedication to a certain set of values. A synonym for *honor* in this context would be *integrity*—"having a keen sense of ethical conduct" as *Webster's* dictionary puts it. The film *Men of Honor* with Cuba Gooding Jr. illustrated this meaning, but I want to get at a different understanding of honor, the primary meaning of *honor* in *Webster's* dictionary: "a good name or public esteem: reputation."

Thomas à Becket served King Henry II of England. As depicted in the film, Becket spent most of his life "improvising" his honor, and he led quite a cynical life of debauchery and unswerving allegiance to his friend-in-vice, the king. This way of life lasted until the king appointed Becket to be leader of the church in England. Once in that role, Becket found himself in a position where he had to make a life-altering choice between the duties of his office and his loyalty to the king. In the crucial scene that reveals his true loyalty and foreshadows his eventual fate, Becket is mocked by his former drinking buddy, the king, for suddenly taking himself seriously in his role as church leader.

The king reminds Becket of the self-serving understanding of honor Becket has employed throughout his life. For Becket to take a principled stand against the king now seems the height of hypocrisy. Becket responds in a humble yet strikingly moving way. He has found an honor worth defending, he explains. The king is outraged. Whose honor could be greater than the king's? Becket responds, "The honor of God."

LIVING FOR THE HONOR OF GOD

Becket decided, finally, that the only honor worth defending was the honor of God. He freed himself from the burden of trying to please everyone, including himself, and chose to follow a calling that the world—and especially the king—could only regard as madness.

Trying to please oneself as well as one's family and friends can be an overwhelming burden. In contrast, Jesus said his yoke is easy (Matt. 11:30). While it might seem to be

> *It is only when the collar and the bit are accepted by the mule that he can receive directions and do useful work.*

the most demanding, depressing, demoralizing, and debilitating thing in the world to try to defend the honor of God—to live as if the good name of God depended on your behavior—in fact, when we take on this "yoke of Christ," we find just the opposite. Thomas à Becket made clear the true nature of things when he said that defending the honor of God was the most freeing thing he had ever experienced.

We sometimes talk about how we want to understand the will of God in our vocational discernment, and we become frustrated when we do not feel leadings, impulses, or sensations directing us in a particular decision. Unfortunately, that expectation is putting the cart before the horse. We have to think of ourselves as being like the lowly mule when it comes to our vocational discernment. Only when the collar goes around the mule's neck is he able to pull anything and therefore be useful. Only when the bit goes in his mouth can he receive directions about which way to go, when to turn, and when to stop. When the mule skinner pulls on the reins, the mule knows where to go. So it is only when the collar and the bit are accepted by the mule that he can receive directions and do useful work.

The primary vocational question, then, is not *What would God have me do?* The true vocational question we all must answer is *Have I accepted the yoke of Christ?* Have I accepted the mule collar around my neck? Have I taken the bit in my mouth so that I can receive the directions God sends me? Am I truly willing to live as if the honor—the good name and reputation—of God depends on who I am in all my living?

> *Our calling from God—to love God and neighbor in a life of agape love that shows forth the fruit of the Spirit—extends beyond any one career.*

Leading a life worthy of our calling does not equate with finding the one job that meets all our needs. Our calling from God—to love God and neighbor in a life of agape love that shows forth the fruit of the Spirit—extends beyond any one career, even (or especially?) the ordained ministry. Statistics point to two peaks in occurrences of suicide over the life cycle: the teenage years and after retirement. That fact demonstrates the stranglehold of the cultural lie "You are what you do" on us. Teenagers, after all, do not yet have a vocational identity (as the world thinks of vocation)—they are not yet a doctor, lawyer, baker; they are not yet "anybody." Similarly, retired people are known primarily by what they *used* to do—who they *used* to be.

Taking a truly Christian understanding of vocation would put all of life into a different perspective. When our vocation means a lifelong movement toward God and becoming more godly—more holy—by deepening in love, joy, peace, and humility—our life has meaning totally independent of the worldly reference scheme of jobs and careers. Our calling as Christians can be lived out and expressed just as clearly through the quality of a look we give our caregivers when a respirator is helping us breathe our last as it can be expressed through the job at which we work for forty years.

On this point I am reminded of a film I made as an undergraduate student. For this forty-five-minute documentary titled "Some Views of God at Carthage College," I asked a variety of faculty and staff the questions *Who or what is God to you?* and *What do you think about when you think about God?* One sociology professor, Dr. Tom Johnson, gave me a reply that still stays with me. In a slightly different way, it expresses what I mean by saying our vocation can be seen as living for the honor of God. Dr. Johnson said that for him, God was the motivation of Jesus.

Jesus' life was lived motivated by God. To understand Jesus' life is to glimpse God. So for us: When we live as if the good name and reputation of God were to be determined by our actions—when we live for the honor of God—God will be seen as our motivation as well. If that is not living for the kingdom of God, I do not know what could be.

The nationally syndicated columnist Marilyn vos Savant, when asked to name the most important human characteristic, answered, "Honor." She said, "Although happiness and success seem to be good goals, the living of a truly honorable life makes the attainment of goals unnecessary."[3] If her secular viewpoint recognizes the truth in living for honor, Becket recognized the true object and source of the only honor worth living for—God.

Christian vocation, then, is not about what we do *for* a living; it is what we do *with* our living. This is the truth of Colossians 3:23, which says, "Whatever your task, put yourselves into it, as done for the Lord," as well as Ephesians 6:7-8: "Render service with enthusiasm, as to the Lord and not to men and women, knowing that whatever good we do, we will receive the same again from the Lord, whether we are slaves or free."

DISCERNING HOW TO LIVE FOR GOD'S HONOR

Many people mistakenly expect discernment about how to live for the honor of God to be a quick and obvious process. In fact, for most people, learning how to express this vocation and live this call requires a period of learning and a period of apprenticeship—sometimes a long apprenticeship. This is nothing new, and in fact, the Bible relates many stories about the necessity of learning how to live for the honor of God.

One such story tells how Moses finds direction for his life at the famous burning bush. When he approaches the burning bush, he has to be told to take his sandals off because he is on holy ground. It was not obvious to Moses that he was in the presence of holiness or what his reaction to it should be—he had to be told. If holiness were not immediately obvious to Moses, why should we expect it to be for us? Should we not expect to have to learn these things at the feet of one who has more experience, more knowledge of the tradition? Yet often we think we should know the best way to live our vocation intuitively, unmediated by any learning process.

Another hero of the Bible who seems somewhat oblivious to the Spirit's nudging is Jacob. After Jacob has a dream revealing (to use my terminology) how he should live for the honor of God, he awakes and says, "Surely the LORD is in this place, and I was not aware of it" (Gen. 28:16, NIV). Again, if one of the patriarchs of the faith was in the presence of God but did not know it, why should we expect such awareness always to be instantly obvious to us, with no process of discernment involved?

The story of Eli and Samuel (1 Samuel 3) also illustrates the need to learn what God's nudging feels like. This story also makes an important point about the communal nature of discernment. Samuel is awakened three times and runs to Eli three times, thinking Eli has called him. Eli finally figures out that God's voice is calling young Samuel, and Samuel finally answers his call and proceeds into his career as a prophet of Yahweh. In several ways, this story parallels the Christian's vocational walk. We need the wisdom and advice of others in the Christian community if we are to discern God's voice truly. The communal nature of the vocational discernment process does not signal shameful individual weakness but our continuing, humble need for the body of Christ, the church on earth.

These stories can also be seen to emphasize the note of freedom in discernment. If we are not looking and listening for discernment and guidance, chances are we will not find it. If we are willing and open—if we have accepted the mule collar of discipleship around our neck—God will find us, God will guide us, and God will show how God's honor can be defended through our life.

CODA: IRONY, WORK, AND VOCATION

This kind of living does entail a kind of dual awareness. We are aware of the particulars of our life immediately at hand—changing diapers, drafting engineering plans, breathing on a ventilator. We also should have another kind of awareness—a program running in the back-

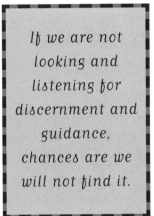

If we are not looking and listening for discernment and guidance, chances are we will not find it.

ground, if you will—an awareness of our calling from God. This double-mindedness can lead us to look for a continued coherence between the two realities, and irony justly arises when we note inconsistency between the two. This means that irony still has its place, as long as it is not the primary idiom of our speech. Only the scoffers and mockers consider irony the primary idiom because they think no way of life could be consonant with the deep desires we hold within us.

Time magazine's 2001 year-end review of all things cultural ranked David Letterman's post–September 11 return to the air as the best television event of the year. With its own columnist's eulogy for irony (quoted above) still a living memory, *Time* allowed that though irony was supposedly "dead," after a self-imposed mourning period, Letterman showed that "topical, cutting satire wasn't just appropriate; it was downright American."[4]

Perhaps we should acknowledge a limited place for the ironic, if not the sarcastic, attitude in the Christian life,

> *After all, the Christian knows the truth of Galatians 6:7: in the end, God will not be mocked.*

especially when it can expose the pretentiousness of any call other than God's, the emptiness of any honor other than God's. The ever-shifting winds of worldly irony and sarcasm can be destructive, but Christians who are clear about God's call—Christians who know where they are going—as Becket did—will be able to push their rudders in the right direction and not let the cultural winds blow them onto a reef or out to sea. Perhaps we Christians who are cast adrift in this culture can even use the power of that irony, by trimming our sails in just the right way, to steer ourselves and others into the safe harbor of God's forgiving and loving grace. After all, the Christian knows the truth of Galatians 6:7: in the end, God will not be mocked.

Like Rick in *Casablanca*, we may want to deny that we are any good at being noble. This avowal may come out of genuine humility—appreciation for God's empowering grace as the truly noble actor; or, it may come out of a worldly sense of wanting to preserve an ironic distance between our actions and our selves. Whatever the motivation for our verbal posturing, ultimately it is important to follow the call and not allow the possibility of being mocked to keep us from living our vocation. A vocation of love that responds to the finite, sinful, and broken world results in our following the Caller's voice all the way home.

QUESTIONS FOR REFLECTION AND DISCUSSION

1. How often do you compare yourself to others? Are such comparisons your primary way of getting a sense of who you are? In your own life, what examples of jealousy's destructiveness do you see?

2. How, by contrast, might an emulating envy lead you to follow the positive example of someone you respect? Think of particular lives you respect and would want to emulate. What is it about them that you would want for your own life? Can you describe the qualities in heart terms; that is, can you name the enviable emotions or spiritual qualities you witness?

3. If you heard the term *honor* in ordinary language, how would you understand it? What picture does the phrase "an honorable man or woman" present to you? If living for the honor of God became the summary goal for your life, what specifically would you feel led to do? What parts of your life would you want to change?

4. How would you go about shaping your life so that it would be consistent with a life lived for the honor of God? How would the life of the church, especially the worship and sacramental life, play a role in this change and your new life agenda? How would living for others be related to living for the honor of God?

5. Who has served as an Eli figure in your life? How, in particular, did that person's discernment help you follow your own calling? How can you serve as an Eli to someone today? Has false modesty or false humility kept you from saying to another, "Listen, that is the voice of God in your life"? How would your life change if you accepted as part of your life agenda helping others discern the call of God in their lives?

CHAPTER **SIX**

"GOD HAS A PLAN FOR YOUR LIFE"
YES, WELL . . .

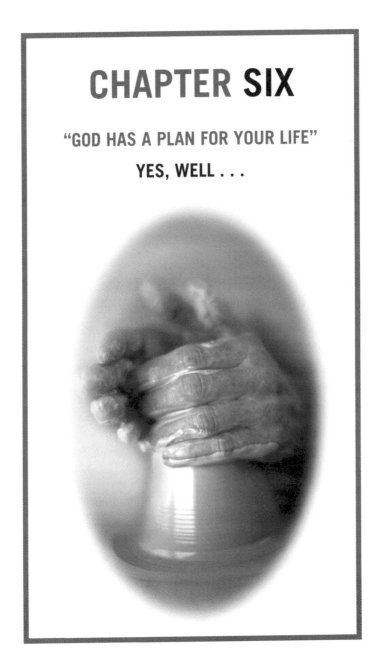

A PERSONAL DISCERNMENT

In a book on Christian vocation, it's tempting to include a section on practical steps for finding a job that matches your talents, gifts, and skills. Many such resources provide such guidance,[1] but I will not try to categorize them or even to summarize their key insights here. If I did, it might reinforce the notion I have been discouraging in this book: that our *job* is the same thing as our *calling* or vocation. Since no career path can ever exhaust the possibilities for leading a life of the fruit of the Spirit, I want to avoid even suggesting it could.

I have decided instead to share my own process of vocational discernment, which includes but is not exhausted by my life in the job market. I do this not because I think my vocational decisions have always been exemplary. Quite the contrary. I share my story because in all my experience in helping people sort out God's call in their lives, it is more typical than not that frustrations, dead-ends, and U-turns mark the way. That has certainly been true for me. It is my hope that sharing my experience may illustrate how, in responding to God's initiating and forgiving love, our freedom can serve the honor of God, even in a world marked at every turn by finitude, sin, brokenness.

Growing up in suburban Chicago, I had a comfortable childhood. In terms of church life, I was baptized, confirmed, and occasionally went to high school youth group. While I experienced some points of deep spiritual connection in the worship services, one of my most vivid memories of encountering God was solitary. Feeling very isolated and lonely at one point as an adolescent, I still sensed that there was a loving presence with me—that I was never truly alone.

As I grew up, I wanted to understand God and the things of God, but I was suspicious that such phenomena could be explained away by rigorous intellectual investigation. When I went to college, I thought perhaps a career as a psychiatrist would offer the capability for answering these mysteries. On entering college, however, my primary focus was *not* on a career or even academics. I wanted to try out for the football team, and that desire consumed most of my energy.

In high school I had played soccer, and my team won the state championship of Illinois without the benefit of my presence on the pitch. I was a bench-rider. But I did have a very strong kicking leg. I practiced kicking footballs all summer before entering college. I was determined to walk on at the University of Wyoming.

When I got to the university, I had a tryout with the head coach of the freshman football team. As one of his assistants held a ball down on the thirty-three-yard line, the coach looked on as I kicked it through the uprights. He held down other balls, and I kicked those through. We moved to the hash marks on the other side of the field, and I knocked several through from there as well. The coach shook my hand and welcomed me to the team. I had made it.

Those who have not participated in sports may regard this achievement as trivial and perhaps unworthy of mention in the present context. I lift it up because being on that team was a milestone for me. I went into a totally foreign place where no one knew me, and I proved myself. This was a real drama for me, and it was unfolding in the right way.

Accordingly, I sympathize when young men tell me, in my present position as a college professor, that they came to college to play baseball or football or basketball. It should be an appalling thing for a professor to hear, but I know the sense of drama and accomplishment that sports can bring. Playing a sport is not the best reason for going to college, but it is a reason.

After four weeks of practice, and just days before our first game of the season, against the Air Force Academy, everything changed. In practice, I typically was by myself or with another kicker doing drills. The defensive backs coach, though, thought that everybody—kickers included—needed their daily "contact"—meaning full-speed collisions with our teammates. I moved over to the practice field and got in some reps at cornerback, a position suited to me since, though light for football, I was fairly fast. I was backpedaling to cover a wide receiver named Steve Washington. As he cut upfield, I pivoted on my left leg to go with him and heard a loud pop. I immediately fell to the ground and started cursing as loudly as I could.

My knee was dislocated, and the patella was stuck on the bone underneath, outside its usual position. My coaches and teammates put me in the back of a pickup truck and took me to the local hospital. There, a nurse took a look at the knee and slapped it back into place, which elicited something other than appreciation on my part, but at least the bone was where it needed to be. Later my knee required surgical reconstruction to avoid repeated dislocation. My season was over. And so was my football career.

After my surgery during Christmas vacation, I found it hard to maneuver the snowy Wyoming campus in winter in a full leg cast. I dropped out of school. When I got home, I worked washing floors at an alcoholic rehabilitation center for several months. This bracing reality motivated me to return to school, and I did the following fall at nearby Carthage College.

At Carthage I decided to play on a club soccer team, which proved to be an appropriate expression of the athletic urge that seemed like a calling at the time. Most of the players were inexperienced, and one year I was named the MVP of the team. I had now come full circle—from bench-rider on a state championship team to MVP on a lousy college team. When those two accomplishments are taken together, it is fair to say that I was a certifiably mediocre soccer player. Though I still enjoy physical activity and also enjoy watching sports, I knew then that I would not find ultimate satisfaction in that area of life. The best expression of my calling did not lie there.

In the classroom at Carthage, psychiatry's medical model of human existence, the one I had thought might hold answers for me, became less attractive. I studied Freud, Jung, and the rising "humanistic" psychologists. It seemed that while psychologists were looking to developmental issues or past traumas as the key to understanding life, they

were ignoring many serious cognitive issues that philosophers were dealing with. My solution was to pursue a
double major in philosophy and psychology.

The summer before my senior year at Carthage, Jody
Rigg and I were married. Looking back on it, I can name this
as an example of following my calling from God. Saying that
is not just a way of "baptizing" that decision in retrospect.
Being married and, later, being the parent of two wonder-
ful daughters, has truly invited me more deeply into the life
of the fruit of the Spirit in ways that I could not have imag-
ined. And I do regard the continuing presence of Jody in my
life as a gracious gift from God. Family life was for me what
sports were not—one way to live out my call from God.

Still, the disciplines of philosophy and psychology had
not met my expectations in terms of answering those pesky
questions about God, so I enrolled in seminary to see
what I might learn there. I entered a master's program not
designed for ordination since I did not feel called into
ordained ministry. After studying for one year while my
wife finished her degree, I was intrigued but also frustrated.
Theology was fascinating, but I felt the pull of the "real
world." As a married man, could I hope to pursue a PhD
and land a teaching job? I faced many years of school and
no guarantee of a job. (Typically more than one hundred
people apply for every college or university teaching position in the humanities.)

Looking back, I confess to a failure of nerve at this point
in my life. I judged the only responsible choice for a married man with my educational background to be that great

promised land of liberal arts graduates: law school. The following fall I enrolled in Marquette University law school.

I studied there a month and could handle the intellectual challenges, but I felt dead inside. I found myself reading philosophy in the evening for fun. My vision of my life after law school made me shudder. While law was an honorable profession that could support a family, I knew it was not for me. Much to my embarrassment, after telling family and friends my intent to be a lawyer, I dropped out of Marquette.

My wife continued to work as a legal secretary while I took a job managing a submarine sandwich store ("Suburpia"). Clearly I didn't want to spend my life doing this, so I looked for a graduate school offering subjects I could pour myself into. I enrolled in a master's program in philosophy at the University of Wisconsin at Milwaukee. Here I found people interested in many of the same questions that interested me, especially Professor William Wainwright, who supervised my comprehensive exams in religious epistemology.

Two experiences profoundly shaped my life when I was in Milwaukee. First, my faith intensified. I cannot call it a conversion because I did identify myself, though tentatively, as a Christian before this experience. But regardless of the terminology used to describe it, something happened.

While changing TV channels one night, I heard a man quote 1 Corinthians 2:5 and say that we must "put our trust in the power of God and not in the wisdom of man." His words went right through me. Here I was studying philosophy, the wisdom of humanity. I had no idea what it might mean to put my trust in the power of God, but I wanted to find out.

Still pondering that issue, within a few weeks I had a sense that if I went to my home church outside Chicago in Park Ridge, I would be led to the next step I should take after my imminent MA graduation. As I drove up to the church, the scripture passage on the bulletin board outside spoke directly to me. On that board were the words "How will they hear if there is no one to preach?" (see Rom. 10:14). Though I did not know exactly what it would mean, I perceived that question as a clear word on how I should live out my call: the ordained ministry. That fall I enrolled at nearby Garrett-Evangelical Theological Seminary—this time in an ordainable program. My first year in seminary did transfer in, so I was able to finish the master of divinity after two more years.

Then my vocational discernment had to intensify again because I still felt pulled toward academia. Put simply, I wanted to understand more and help others understand. I did not know whether this leaning could be consistent with my call into ordained ministry, but I knew that both these pulls felt real. My ordination as a deacon in The United Methodist Church helped me live with both pulls and not try to suppress one or the other. At the ordination ceremony, the bishop who preached, Bishop Choy, said something that has stayed with me to this day. While it was a beautiful thing to be called to ordained ministry and something to celebrate, he said, this call might not be the end of our professional decision making. He said that one day God may call us out of the ordained ministry.

The comment angered some at the ceremony. We had just come through an intense period of discernment, prayer,

> *Pursuing a PhD, even with my sense of confirmation, still seemed like a huge leap of faith.*

counseling, and education, and now the bishop was suggesting . . . what? That being ordained could be a mistake? Some heard him that way, but that was not his point. The bishop was suggesting that living out our call can never be exhausted through an occupational commitment— not even a commitment to serve in the church full-time. His observation freed me to be true to the intellectual restlessness pulling me toward academic pursuits.

As I was finishing my master of divinity degree, I applied to graduate programs and was accepted into two. My decision was not final, though, until I got word of receiving a three-year fellowship to cover tuition and expenses. When that came through, my wife and I agreed that pursuing this PhD was the best way to express my calling.

Pursuing a PhD, even with my sense of confirmation, still seemed like a huge leap of faith. After all, the job market had not changed since I was scared into attending law school; I might very well pour years into earning this degree only to end up never teaching. But Jody and I stared at this uncertainty, prayed, and jumped into it.

While I studied at Emory and Jody worked as a secretary, we decided to become parents. It was not a case of pressure from our parents or peer pressure or a biological accident. At some level, we wanted to participate more fully in life, though that sounds a bit formal and stuffy when I put it on paper. Looking back, I see that step in our lives as a way of expressing our vocation—choosing to be in relationships of love with people—not people in general but specific creatures of God whom we could help to bring into the world.

If finishing my PhD was a milestone for me professionally, being home half of each day to help raise my daughters was just as important for me as a human being, a person trying to follow God's voice back to its source. In both activities I felt like I was living consistent with my vocation.

As I approached the end of my study at Emory, I began to see how my training might be put to use for God's kingdom. I had been teaching at a nearby United Methodist church and had become acquainted with the senior pastor, Garnett Wilder. He knew about my search for a full-time college teaching position, but he also knew the odds against my landing one. He said that if I did not receive an offer to teach, I could join his staff as an associate minister. At the last minute, though, just before graduation, I received an offer to teach at Westmar College, a United Methodist school in Le Mars, Iowa. Garnett's offer could have led me to a career using my freedom in the local church. His offer did not seem to be just a nice fall-back job but a positive, enlivening option. Sometimes our vocational choices are not between good and bad options. Rather, they come down to choosing which of several good soils can grow the best fruit.

While I was filled with excitement about teaching and was grateful for the opportunity, moving to northwest Iowa with a wife and two small children was not an entirely attractive adventure. Teaching at a tiny school that nobody had ever heard of did not seem very glamorous or flattering to my ego either. In addition, doing the work of a theologian—teaching and writing—was hardly the kind of direct amelioration of suffering that parish ministry can entail. But I knew that ignorance and confusion can bring their own kind of suffering, and I thought that addressing them through teaching religion and philosophy seemed an absolutely delightful way for me to express my calling. We made the move, and for five years it was a wonderfully satisfying life.

While at Westmar, though I loved the teaching, I felt a need to live out my call beyond the classroom as well. That prompted me to join the Iowa Air National Guard as a chaplain. The part-time military ministry seemed to be a perfect complement to my academic work. On campus I interacted with primarily traditional college-age students, while once a month I interacted with a much broader spectrum of people and a much broader spectrum of concerns and issues. I felt myself positively pulled and expanded in a number of different areas, especially when United Flight 232 crashed at our air base, and I was called into ministry in the midst of the aftermath. I wrote about those events in *When the World Breaks Your Heart: Spiritual Ways of Living with Tragedy*. That ministry was a part of answering God's call in my life.

During my fifth year at Westmar, the school was absorbed by a Japanese university. In a desire to attract a lot of (full-tuition-paying) international students, Westmar's administration agreed to a deal that amounted to a full takeover by the Japanese school. In my sixth year at Westmar, I had a choice to make. At that point the takeover had become final, and it became clear that The United Methodist Church would disaffiliate with the new university because it would not allow seats on the board of trustees to church officials. I had just been promoted and granted tenure, and I faced a fundamental choice. If I saw myself primarily as an academic, I should stay; if I saw myself as primarily related to the church, I should leave.

The school's difficulties during transition added confusion to my situation: my sabbatical was promised, then canceled. But then a clear invitation came my way from United Methodist district superintendent Marvin Arnpriester. Would I be interested in the position of senior pastor at a church near the University of Northern Iowa, the school my wife wanted to attend?

I felt this position, though not an academic post, called me to the next right step in my vocation. We moved to Waverly, even though we knew getting back into academia after stepping outside it could be very difficult. I knew that preaching, teaching, and administering in a local church was what I was supposed to do next. At the end of my third year in that position, the Staff-Parish Relations Committee unanimously wanted me back for the foreseeable future. At the same time, I received notice of an academic opening that seemed suited to me.

One reality had become evident about parish life: all the rich interactions with people left no time to write. An academic position, with its nine-month schedule and regular sabbaticals, could provide that time, and I did feel writing was an important part of being true to God's call in my life. I accepted the position of associate professor in the Chapman Benson chair of Christian Faith and Philosophy at Huntingdon College in Montgomery, Alabama.

An attractive feature of this position was the stipulation to lead continuing-education events for local clergy. Thus I could maintain my strong church connection at this United Methodist–related school. In addition, the college curriculum incorporated a strong requirement in religion. All students had to take both Old and New Testament—a year of Bible—highly unusual, especially for a United Methodist college.

Sounds good, right? It was for four years. Then the faculty revamped its curriculum and dropped the Bible requirements. In the new plan, I could teach such courses as introduction to liberal arts, beginning writing courses, and the occasional religion course. That scenario did not match what I felt God was calling me to, so once again I waded into the treacherous waters of the academic job market.

The University of Indianapolis had just received a grant from the Lilly Endowment to start one of the first programs in the area of Christian vocation. The school was searching for someone to help run it and to teach in the philosophy and religion department. Even though it meant moving my family again, my wife and I decided that this was the next step in following God's call back to its source. We moved to the Indianapolis area.

At the University of Indianapolis I was promoted to full professor and given tenure. After the vocation grant ran out,

I eventually moved over to teaching full-time in the philosophy and religion department.

Was that the last of my career moves? From a human standpoint, my wife and I both certainly hope so! Finally, the best answer, the only answer I can give about the future, from the perspective of looking back on my professional life, is to say only God knows.

Wherever I may be led in following God's call, and to

> *The joke is on us at those times when we find out that our faithfulness leads to what we truly want in our heart of hearts after all.*

whatever task, I trust in the grace that has shown itself in all the unexpected roller-coaster rides of my life. In the midst of my sometimes incomplete discernment and my failures of nerve, in the midst of the limitations on freedom that come from finitude, sin, and brokenness, God is faithful. Mustering a response of faithful service can at times seem like a sacrifice. However, the joke is on us at those times when we find out that our faithfulness leads to what we truly want in our heart of hearts after all—a life marked by love, joy, peace, and all the fruit of the Spirit.

Being faithful in our broken and bruised world is a plan less precise than a treasure map, where a dotted line leads to the spot marked "X." Nonetheless, it is a plan that will occasionally shine forth a bit of the honor of God. If I am faithful in remembering God's love and forgiveness

> "I choose to hold within my heart the image of Christ and to strive to grow into that image more each day."

and acting out of humble gratitude, this plan finally will lead me home.

Let me share a simple motto for the Christian life composed by Susie Peach Foster. Miss Foster served as a Methodist missionary to Korea for ten years before World War II, then as director of a Wesley Foundation on a college campus. She was a civil rights worker in the South at a time when that kind of work could bear a heavy cost. She also told hilarious monologues and stories.

The pledge was discovered by her niece, Kate Lindsey, in the papers Susie Peach left behind. Kate took it to her Sunday school class, where the pledge became a weekly recitation. I learned it when I joined that class during our time in Alabama. It still echoes in my heart.

> I choose to hold within my heart the image of Christ
> and to strive to grow into that image more each day.

We have already been given the image of Christ, and now our job is to use our will, energy, and freedom to grow into it. To me, this pledge summarizes our calling, and I pray that we all will follow our calling through the twists and turns of life as clearly as Susie Peach did.

In the Introduction, I recalled the poised and ready posture of the *Star Wars* soldiers about to meet the challenge on the other side of the door. I invite you to look to that door now, whatever its shape and location in your life at the present time. It may be a looming layoff or retirement. It may be graduation or a new job. It may be the approaching end of your life on earth. Whatever lies on the other side, know that it is nothing that has not already been conquered by the crucified and risen Christ. Most importantly, nothing on the other side of that door can separate you from the love of God, and nothing can keep you from a response of faith, hope, and love when you are open to the guidance of the Spirit.

QUESTIONS FOR REFLECTION AND DISCUSSION

1. Consider writing your own spiritual autobiography—your own narration of how you have said yes or no to God's call at various times in your life. What have been key turning points? Are there any crises to recount, or were there instead long periods of faithfulness as you moved steadily in one direction? Perhaps you've encountered both. Start making a few notes, then see if they start to grow into something longer. Imagine this work as something that you would want to give your grandchildren as a truthful view of how God's grace and your freedom intersected in your life. See it as a work that might help them accept and face their brokenness, finitude, and sinfulness with a calm assurance of God's love and a determination to use their freedom in creative and loving ways.

2. Have you ever considered taking notes on vocational discernment for someone else's life? If you have children, grandchildren, or young friends and relatives, observe how they live out God's call in their lives. You could gather those notes in an album for a graduation or birthday gift. On a smaller scale, make a resolution to take note when you see one of your friends saying yes to God's call, then acknowledge it to that person, perhaps in a short, handwritten letter. Chances are you will be surprised at the long-term effects these little acts of discernment can have in the lives you touch.

3. In the Susie Peach Foster pledge, the emphasis rests on *choosing, striving,* and *growing,* underlining the reality that our part in God's kingdom entails active and conscious commitments. How might you embody this pledge to express the image of Christ in your life today, given your particular current challenges and burdens? How could you choose to embody the image of Christ in your work, in your home, with your friends, at your church?

NOTES

CHAPTER 1

1.   (Nashville, Tenn.: Word Publishing, 1998), 43.

2.   On this point of emphasizing God's call as being a *relationship* and not primarily to a particular job or location, see not only Guinness's book but also *The Fabric of This World: Inquiries into Calling* by Lee Hardy (Grand Rapids, Mich.: W. B. Eerdmans, 1990) and *The Way of Life: A Theology of Christian Vocation* by Gary Badcock (Grand Rapids, Mich.: W. B. Eerdmans, 1998), as well as Rowan Williams's essay on vocation in his *Open to Judgement: Sermons and Addresses* (London: Darton, Longman and Todd Ltd., 1994), 171–77, and *Courage and Calling* by Gordon T. Smith (Downer's Grove, Ill.: InterVarsity, 1999). Miroslav Volf's book on work makes a similar point, though he urges abandonment of the term *vocation* altogether in favor of emphasizing the charisms—gifts of the Spirit. See his *Work in the Spirit: Toward a Theology of Work* (New York: Oxford University Press, 1991), 107 ff. This wide vision of vocation's meaning is also evident in *The Catechism of the Catholic Church* (Liberia Editrice Vaticana/United States Catholic Conference, 1997), specifically in "Our Vocation of Beatitude," pp. 426 ff.

3.   The image of "breaking the crust" first came to me in reading M. Robert Mulholland's excellent book on reading scripture for spiritual formation, *Shaped by the Word: The Power of Scripture in Spiritual Formation*, rev. ed. (Nashville, Tenn.: Upper Room Books, 2000).

4.   *Time* 154, no. 27 (December 31, 1999), 135.

5.   (Boston: Little, Brown and Company, 1951), 224–25.

6.   In a secular setting, we can see this truth reflected in George W. Bush's 2001 inaugural address when he said, "We find the fullness of life not only in options but in commitments."

7.   For one eloquent advocate of simplicity, see Richard J. Foster's *Celebration of Discipline 20th Anniversary: The Path to Spiritual Growth* (San Francisco: HarperSanFrancisco, 2003), especially chapter 6, "Simplicity."

8.   In *Heroism and the Christian Life: Reclaiming Excellence,* the authors, Brian S. Hook and Russell R. Reno, reinforce my perception of the relationship between jadedness and denying our vocation when they assert

that the "cynical suspicions" of our culture reinforce the sense that normalcy and comfortable survival are goals enough for ordinary folk (Louisville, Ky.: Westminster John Knox Press, 2000), 212 ff.

9. (September 24, 2001):79.

10. Lance Morrow, "Is This Still Frank Capra's America?" *Time*, January 14, 2002, 70.

11. See Theodore W. Jennings Jr., *Good News to the Poor: John Wesley's Evangelical Economics* (Nashville, Tenn.: Abingdon Press, 1990), especially pp. 53 ff. This dynamic is why "service learning" is becoming increasingly popular on church-related college campuses. Deep, experiential learning does take place in the practice of service, more so than from reading or talking about an issue.

12. For example, films such as *Groundhog Day*, where the jaded weatherman Phil literally gets stuck in a rut—a rut of time—until he starts living for others; or *About a Boy*, where the leading character discovers that letting the suffering of others make a difference in his life opens him up to the true richness of life. See also Jedediah Purdy's book *For Common Things: Irony, Trust, and Commitment in America Today* (New York: Knopf, 1999), where he analyzed the uncommitted "whatever" generation portrayed in the television series *Seinfeld* and found that this generation of young people is looking for something more than the empty glibness depicted in that show.

Chapter 2

1. (Notre Dame: University of Notre Dame Press, 2000).

2. See Meilaender's introductory essay in *Working*, in which he shows how some thinkers have seen leisure not as rest but as intrinsically worthwhile activity. Later in this essay, he shows how this might be related to worship. See pp. 4–7 and 20–23. Further intriguing discussions of the nature of leisure can also be found in David Steindl-Rast's *Gratefulness, the Heart of Prayer: An Approach to Life in Fullness* (New York: Paulist Press, 1984), chapter 4, "Contemplation and Leisure," as well as in Os Guinness's *The Call: Finding and Fulfilling the Central Purpose of Your Life*, chapter 4, "Everyone, Everywhere, Everything," especially pp. 32–36.

3. See note 2, chapter 1.

Notes

Chapter 3

1. See passages such as Acts 4:28; Romans 8:29-30; and Ephesians 1:4-14. While on the face of it, these passages seem to say that God does set all of history out in advance, theologians have argued about the *basis* for this predestination. Should we understand God as causing all these actions, or did God foresee who would have faith and then predestine them? Even such "obvious" scriptures, then, do not free us from the making of hard choices about how to use our freedom.

2. Portions of what follows were first published in "From the 'Works of the Flesh' to the 'Fruit of the Spirit': Conversion and Spiritual Formation in the Wesleyan Tradition," a chapter I wrote for *Conversion in the Wesleyan Tradition,* edited by Kenneth J. Collins and John H. Tyson (Nashville, Tenn.: Abingdon Press, 2001), 211–22.

3. On this point, see also Lieutenant Dan's often-wrong hunches about where the enemy was when he was out on patrols. His metaphysical sense of what lay before him was quite fallible.

Chapter 4

1. "Not That Different," written by Karen Taylor-Good and Joie Scott, copyright 1995 W.B.M./K.T. Good Music (SESAC)/Spoofer Music (BMI).

2. To name only two examples, the following are quite different but equally helpful works: *Life on the Vine: Cultivating the Fruit of the Spirit in Christian Community* by Philip D. Kenneson (Downers Grove, Ill.: InterVarsity Press, 1999) and *The Workbook on Virtues and the Fruit of the Spirit* by Maxie Dunnam and Kimberly Dunnam Reisman (Nashville, Tenn.: Upper Room Books, 1998).

3. See my *John Wesley on Religious Affections: His Views on Experience and Emotion and Their Role in the Christian Life and Theology* (Metuchen: Scarecrow Press, 1989). For two contemporary philosophers' analyses of emotion, see *A Tear Is an Intellectual Thing* by Jerome Neu (Oxford: Oxford University Press, 2002) and *Upheavals of Thought* by Martha C. Nussbaum (Cambridge: Cambridge University Press, 2001).

4. For one specific example, see Richard Rorty, *Philosophy and the Mirror of Nature* (Princeton, N.J.: Princeton University Press, 1981).

5. See, for example, *Upheavals of Thought* by Martha C. Nussbaum (Cambridge: Cambridge University Press, 2001).

6. See William H. Willimon's good overview of baptism, *Remember Who You Are: Baptism, a Model for Christian Life* (Nashville, Tenn.: Upper Room Books, 1988).

7. From "Prayer of Humble Access," Word and Table: Service IV, in *The United Methodist Hymnal* (Nashville, Tenn.: The United Methodist Publishing House, 1989), 30.

8. For this dynamic see also the film *Field of Dreams* where the ballplayers sometimes stop and ask, "Is this heaven?" When we step out in faith, we can catch glimpses of heaven on earth.

CHAPTER 5

1. Immanuel Kant, "Jealousy, Envy, and Spite," trans. Louis Enfield, in *Vice and Virtue in Everyday Life: Introductory Readings in Ethics,* 5th ed., edited by Christina Sommers and Fred Sommers (Fort Worth, Tex.: Harcourt College Publishers, 2001), 405.

2. Ibid.

3. *Parade*, February 12, 1995.

4. *Time* 158, no. 27 (December 24, 2001):83.

CHAPTER 6

1. See, for example, the classic in the field: *What Color Is Your Parachute?* by Richard Nelson Bolles (Berkeley, Calif.: Ten Speed Press, 2003).

ABOUT THE AUTHOR

GREGORY S. CLAPPER is professor of religion and philosophy at
the University of Indianapolis. He was one of two founding
directors of the Lantz Center for Christian Vocations there,
initially funded by a grant from the Lilly Endowment.

A graduate of Carthage College, Greg Clapper received
an MA in philosophy from the University of Wisconsin at
Milwaukee and an MDiv from Garrett-Evangelical Theological Seminary. He earned a PhD from Emory University. He
completed the Upper Room's Academy for Spiritual Formation and Walk to Emmaus.

Greg Clapper has authored numerous articles and pub-
lished two other books with Upper Room Books: *When the
World Breaks Your Heart: Spiritual Ways of Living with
Tragedy* and *As If the Heart Mattered: A Wesleyan Spirituality.*